Western Approaches
to the Soviet Union

Gregory Treverton

Pierre Hassner

Edwina Moreton

Stanley Hoffmann

Michael Mandelbaum, editor

Council on Foreign Relations
New York

COUNCIL ON FOREIGN RELATIONS BOOKS

The Council on Foreign Relations, Inc., is a nonprofit and nonpartisan organization devoted to promoting improved understanding of international affairs through the free exchange of ideas. The Council does not take any position on questions of foreign policy and has no affiliation with, and receives no funding from, the United States government.

From time to time, books and monographs written by members of the Council's research staff or visiting fellows, or commissioned by the Council, or written by an independent author with critical review contributed by a Council study or working group are published with the designation "Council on Foreign Relations Book." Any book or monograph bearing that designation is, in the judgment of the Committee on Studies of the Council's board of directors, a responsible treatment of a significant international topic worthy of presentation to the public. All statements of fact and expressions of opinion contained in Council books are, however, the sole responsibility of the author.

Library of Congress Cataloging-in-Publication Data

Western approaches to the Soviet Union / Gregory F. Treverton . . . [et al.].
  p. cm.
ISBN 0-87609-048-X
1. Europe—Foreign relations—Soviet Union. 2. Soviet Union—Foreign relations—
Europe. 3. Europe—Foreign relations—1945-   I. Treverton, Gregory F.
D1065.S65W47 1988
327.4047—dc 19   88-39780
                                                                          CIP

Contents

Acknowledgements

This volume is part of the Council on Foreign Relations Project on East-West Relations. The Project is supported by the Carnegie Corporation, and this volume was made possible, in part, by a grant from the Ford Foundation.

Preliminary versions of the chapters were presented to a conference at the Council on September 28 and 29, which was chaired by Stanley Hoffmann. The authors and the editor are grateful to those who took part in the conference for their comments and suggestions, and to Cynthia Paddock for organizing it.

Introduction

Michael Mandelbaum

For forty years the single most important feature of international politics has been the confrontation of two powerful military and political blocs. The Eastern bloc is a Russian-dominated empire, a descendant of the Hapsburg, Ottoman, and Romanov dynasties that once held sway in the eastern and southern parts of the continent. The Western bloc is a coalition that was organized to offset the Soviet Union. It is descended from the coalitions formed to oppose would-be hegemonic powers in Europe in the past—the France of Louis XIV and Napoleon and the Germany of Wilhelm II and Hitler.

The formal military structure of the Western coalition is the North Atlantic Treaty Organization. It is loosely affiliated with countries in other parts of the world—Japan and South Korea, for example—that are allied with the United States and opposed to the Soviet Union. At the core of the Western bloc, however, are the four countries whose policies are central to this volume: the Federal Republic of Germany, the United States, France, and Great Britain.

Soviet troops occupy the other member countries of the Eastern bloc. The Western coalition, by contrast, is a voluntary association. Its members have similar forms of government and extensive economic dealings with one another. What unites them, however, and forms the basis of the Western Alliance for its most important members, is a common view of the Soviet Union.

Since the late 1940s each of the four has regarded the Soviet Union as a potential military threat. Each has therefore believed that its security depended on the existence of a powerful counterweight to the Soviet forces in Europe. All have agreed that checking Moscow's expansionist ambitions in the West requires a firm American commitment to the defense of Western Europe and a military strategy involving nuclear weapons, principally American ones.

Although all four countries have subscribed to these basic precepts, their views of the Soviet Union and indeed their policies toward their common adversary have by no means been uniform. The differences among them are typical of alliances. Although alliances are partnerships, although the parties to them agree on a few important matters, they seldom agree on everything.

So it has been with the Western Alliance. Even on the very issue that gave rise to it, policy toward the Soviet Union, its most important members have differed. Those differences—past, present, and future—are the subjects of this book.

Allies agree on whom to oppose but not always on how to do so. The necessary condition for an alliance is a consensus on a political goal; its members can, and often do, differ on the military measures best suited to attain it. Those differences will reflect varying political interests and, most importantly, the inevitable disagreement among allies over how to distribute the costs of achieving their common goal.

This is true in wartime. The allies who fought Hitler disagreed on the question of a second front in Europe—that is on where and when the United States and Great Britain would move their forces onto the continent. This was a dispute about, among other things, how many casualties each country would have to bear to win the war.

A comparable disagreement is part of the history of the Western Alliance in the postwar period. It concerns the role of nuclear weapons in the Alliance's military strategy. The United States has periodically sought to put greater emphasis on nonnuclear forces than has been acceptable to the Europeans, who have generally insisted on relying heavily on American nuclear arms. At one level this has been a dispute about what kind of threat would most effectively deter a Soviet attack on Western Europe. The Europeans have wished to rely on nuclear weapons on the grounds that a nuclear war would be so horrible for all concerned that the Soviet Union would never dare launch an attack if it were assured that such an attack would trigger a nuclear conflict. The United States has wanted the Alliance to be capable of waging a nonnuclear conflict on the continent on the theory that nuclear war would be so catastrophic that a Western threat to initiate one lacked credibility and thus might fail to deter Moscow.

At another level, however, this was a debate about costs—in both resources and human lives. A nonnuclear war would be fought in Europe, and perhaps Europe alone; a nuclear war would almost certainly involve North America.

The members of the coalition have also disagreed about how to apportion the costs of preparing for war. How many troops, tanks, and airplanes each country would contribute to the common effort have been a source of continuing contention. This should not be surprising:

for an alliance of sovereign states, defense is what economists call a "public good." All parties agree that it is necessary, but none is anxious to volunteer to pay a large share of its costs. This is precisely how taxpayers within municipalities traditionally regard public goods such as police and fire protection.

The heart of any alliance is not its military strategy but its political purpose. Allies will coalesce politically to the extent that the threat they face seems pressing. To the extent, by contrast, that the threat eases, other interests come to the fore.

The coalitions that won the great wars of the last two centuries, the Napoleonic Wars and World Wars I and II, dissolved in the wake of victory. The alliance that defeated Hitler collapsed abruptly and with considerable bitterness. The United States and the Soviet Union had a common interest in defeating Germany but once that was accomplished their interests were not only no longer identical, they turned out to be opposed.

Nothing quite as dramatic as the victory over Germany has occurred in the postwar period. The Soviet Union remains a threat, but to the members of the Alliance the urgency of the threat that it poses has declined. This was not the result of a single event or a particular moment. Rather, between the early 1960s, with the Berlin crisis of 1961 and the Cuban missile crisis of 1962, when war between the two blocs seemed near, and the early 1970s, with the signing of the German accords in 1971 and the first SALT agreements in 1972, the conviction took hold in the West that the military balance was stable. While the political conflict would continue, the four principal members of the Alliance all came to believe the Soviet side was unlikely to wage the struggle in military terms. Moscow's intervention in Czechoslovakia in 1968 demonstrated that the most dangerous and objectionable features of the Soviet political system were still very much alive; but the events in Prague that August never threatened to embroil the West. At the end of this ten-year period war seemed, if not impossible, then highly unlikely.

If the Soviet Union has ceased to be an immediate threat, this means that the Allies have some latitude in dealing with Moscow on the basis of their different national experiences and interests. Those differences are analyzed in the chapters of this book.

The four countries occupy different geographical and political positions, which make for different national perceptions, responsibilities, and aspirations among them. These have given rise, in turn, to dissimilar policies toward the Soviet Union. The most basic distinction is between the two countries—the Federal Republic of Germany and the United States—that have the most direct connections with the Soviet Union and the other two—France and Great Britain—whose interactions with Moscow are less pronounced.

The Federal Republic, as Gregory Treverton notes in his essay, is NATO's "front-line state." Its eastern border is the boundary between the Eastern and Western blocs. The war that the two armies are poised to fight would be a war in and for Germany. The Federal Republic has another, equally important, connection with Moscow. The Soviet Union actually occupies part of Germany. Twenty divisions of the Soviet Army are stationed in the German Democratic Republic, enforcing the division of the country.

In the 1970s, Bonn developed a new strategy for dealing with the division of Germany. Its policy of "reassociation" has sought to increase the human contacts between the two German states. It is within the power of the Soviet Union to block the trade, loans, and visits between the two Germanies that have developed over the past two decades and that the Federal Republic has attempted to foster. West Germany thus has an abiding interest in good relations with Moscow. Its Soviet policy has an implicit bias toward conciliation.

For the United States, by contrast, as is described in Stanley Hoffmann's essay, the Soviet Union is a global rival. Washington confronts Moscow not only in Europe but in the rest of the world and in an ongoing military competition as well. Thus the United States has felt the need to respond to developments outside Europe that mean far less to the Europeans. The Soviet military buildup of the 1970s and the invasion of Afghanistan in 1979 evoked a sharper response in Washington than in the capitals of Western Europe. The bias of American policy toward the Soviet Union is toward confrontation.

France is more detached from the East-West conflict than either West Germany or the United States. In the 1960s, Charles de Gaulle was the first Western leader to assume the stability of the military balance in Europe and to act on that assumption. Since war was ruled out, France's relations with the Soviet Union could be put at the service of what became the country's principal international aim—to maximize France's independence, and independent influence, in the international arena.

In military terms this involved maintaining an independent French nuclear force. France has asserted its political independence by initiating relations with Moscow that were separate from and more cordial than those of the other three Western powers in the 1960s. Since then, as Pierre Hassner's essay records, the French approach to

Moscow has varied, often running deliberately counter to the prevailing trend in East-West relations.

Like France, Great Britain has fewer direct connections with the Soviet Union than either the Federal Republic or the United States. Like the French, the British have sought to maximize their own influence. Unlike the French, as Edwina Moreton's survey of British policy toward the Soviet Union demonstrates, the British have invariably sought to accomplish this goal not through independent policies but in cooperation with the other Western powers—first the United States during the time of the "special relationship" between Washington and London from the end of the war through the early 1960s and more recently through the Alliance as a whole. The British approach to the Soviet Union has consistently relied on a multilateral framework.

To the extent that the threat that first united them becomes less immediate, differences about how to deal with the adversary are likely to emerge within as well as among the member states of an alliance. So it has been with the Western Alliance. Indeed, since all four countries are democracies, internal, partisan disagreement is not only common, it is inevitable. Indeed it has been institutionalized in each of them.

The degree to which domestic politics, and therefore domestic divisions, affect foreign policy varies among the four. Foreign policy is most nearly isolated from domestic politics in France; at the other end of the spectrum, domestic affairs in the United States impinge most forcefully on relations with other countries. On this dimension of political life, Germany and Britain fall between the other two.

On occasion, internal divisions in one or another of the four powers over how to deal with the Soviet Union have been particularly important. In the 1970s they were perhaps sharpest in Germany, where the Christian Democrats rejected the governing Social Democrats' policy toward the East. In the first half of the 1980s the internal differences were most acute in the United States, where Republicans and Democrats were at odds over *détente* and arms control. In the 1990s, the divisions may become widest in Britain, where the Labor and Conservative parties diverge not so much on the appropriate political approach to the Soviet Union as on the Alliance's defense strategy and whether Britain ought to have its own nuclear weapons.

In general, the differences in approach to the Soviet Union among the four principal members of the Western Alliance are likely to diverge even farther in the 1990s. This is because of the reform program within the Soviet Union of General Secretary Mikhail Gorbachev.

In the history of the Alliance there have been two great turning points, two developments that defined the threat that the West faced and thus the nature of the differences among them. The first development, between 1945 and 1949, was the beginning of the Cold War. The Soviet Union was deemed a threat; the differences that followed among the Allies concerned military strategy. The second, between 1962 and 1972, was the easing of the military threat that Moscow was thought to pose, which paved the way for the political divergencies of the last two decades.

The Gorbachev program has the potential to be a third such turning point. The changes that he has inaugurated bear not just on Soviet foreign policy but on the character of the Soviet political system itself. They are therefore likely to affect not only Western perceptions of the urgency of the military threat posed by the Soviet Union but also the very nature of that threat. This, in turn, could accentuate the differences that already exist among the four principal allies, or create new ones, or both.

Each author speculates, at the end of his or her essay, about the future of the Soviet policy of the country in question, and the possible effects of Gorbachev and his program on it. It is on these effects that the shape of the Western Alliance in the 1990s is likely to depend.

Western Approaches
to the Soviet Union

§

West Germany and the Soviet Union

Gregory F. Treverton

The structural features that define Western Europe's current position are now so much taken for granted that it is easy to lose sight of their effect. They all bear most heavily on the Federal Republic; in this respect, as in others, Germany is the "heart" of Europe.[1] In coming to depend on alliance with the United States and on American nuclear weapons as the ultimate deterrent of Soviet power, the European states reacquired all the attributes of sovereignty save the most crucial one—responsibility for national defense. Hence it is no surprise that dependence has been frustrating to European elites and occasionally terrifying to people in the street, nor that the dependence has become gradually more chafing as the Europeans have become the economic equals of the United States. Indeed, dependence may be all the more uncomfortable precisely because there is little apparent alternative to it.

For the Federal Republic, the discomfort is triple: as the forward area—the "central front," in curiously evocative NATOese—it is the most exposed country. As a divided state, Germany has the greatest stake in the condition of East-West relations, but its stake is not matched by commensurate influence, for many of the levers of influence still reside in the hands of the superpowers. As divided and denuclearized, it is the most dependent despite having the largest army in central Europe.

These structural circumstances are the background to the Federal Republic's relations with the United States and the Western Alliance. For instance, the fact that public opinion polls record strong support for NATO but strong doubt about its strategy or the wisdom of stationing more nuclear weapons on German soil seems, at first blush, paradoxical.[2] At second glance it is not: buying some insurance against Soviet military power through NATO seems sensible, but being

1

reminded of Germany's place as the likely battleground should deterrence fail is hardly appealing. Neither is having the nuclear weapons that might do the battle based, figuratively, in one's living room.

So, for all the durability of its Western link, there is a certain brittleness to it; minor perturbations produce visible cracks. Germany suffers in most extreme form from the dilemma of the dependent—either abandonment or entrapment.[3] The dependent ally may be abandoned in two quite different ways—either through the superpower reneging on its commitments at the ally's hour of greatest need or through the superpowers conniving over the head of the ally to the neglect of its interests. The opposite fear, entrapment, derives from the possibility that the dependent ally will be dragged into a conflict by its patron against its will and with damage to its interests.

One or other of these twin fears may predominate at particular times or with regard to particular issues. For the Federal Republic, for instance, recent policy seems an attempt to sustain "coupling" in Europe—that is, a tolerable degree of American commitment to the core German interest in counterbalancing Soviet power on the continent—while "decoupling" Germany from the United States in areas beyond Europe.

The issue for this chapter is whether anything has changed or is changing. In particular, is change afoot in West German attitudes toward the Soviet Union, in the domestic politics surrounding those attitudes and in the policies that emanate from those attitudes and politics? And if so, what are the implications for the United States and the North Atlantic alliance, broadly construed—that is, not just NATO but the broader web of economic and political cooperation?

The Legacy of History

In the history of the postwar period the position of Germany has been exceptional. This is so not so much because of the division of the country per se. There have always been several German states comprising the German nation, particularly during the German confederation (*Bund*) of the nineteenth century. (In more recent times, François Mauriac remarked that he liked Germany so much he was happy there were two—now three, if Austria is included.) Now, as then, Germans can be nationalists without necessarily being unifiers.[4]

Rather, what is unusual is the extent of the Western tug on the biggest part of Germany, the Federal Republic. In that sense, Germany is now more "Western" than it has been since the Holy Roman Empire.

The loss of East Germany left the Federal Republic more Catholic than the Germany that Bismarck created and dominated by the part that had historically been closest to the West, especially France. Konrad Adenauer, in particular, had always been drawn westward. It is said that as mayor of Cologne from 1917 to 1920 and then as president of the Prussian State Council, he had always felt some hesitation in crossing the Elbe eastward.[5]

This is not the place to rehearse German history, but several points will serve to demonstrate just how exceptional the postwar period has been. One such point, trivial but easy to understate, is the tradition of European, and especially German, statecraft as a reflection of the state's interests, not passions or ideologies. The famous quote from Bismarck captures the essence of what later came to be called *Realpolitik:*

> Sympathies and antipathies with respect to foreign Powers and persons I cannot justify to my sense of duty to the foreign service of my country. . . . Therein lies the embryo of disloyalty toward one's master or the land one serves . . . In my view, not even the King has the right to subordinate the interests of the fatherland to personal feelings of love and hate toward the foreigner. . . .[6]

In this spirit, conservative, anti-Communist German diplomats made the 1922 Rapallo agreement with the Soviet Union, and thus created "Rapallo" as the West's catchword for German unreliability. They did so because they believed their state's interests required it.

For Americans, *Realpolitik* has come to connote amorality in foreign affairs. For Germans, however, the observation that they share the continent with the Soviet Union is more than a simple commentary on geography; for them the crusading moralism of American policy, the opposite of *Realpolitik*, is dumbfounding and sometimes frightening, whether the crusade is Wilsonian internationalism or Reaganite anticommunism.

Realpolitik is linked to another historical tradition, also common to Europe but also, perhaps, strongest in Germany—the relative isolation of foreign policy from domestic politics. Before 1919 the United States was a democracy and Germany was not; Bismarck was more constrained by the preeminent role of the military than by the interplay of interests, passions, and ideas common to democratic societies. Both the role of the military and the discretion for the government continued into the Weimar period and, needless to say, during the Third Reich.

In the modern Federal Republic, a parliamentary system, the Bundestag's committees of foreign affairs are weak. Memories of

Weimar instability influenced the drafting of a constitution that sets high hurdles for the entry into parliament of minority parties. Moreover, habits of discipline matter as much as constitutional forms: in the early 1980s, protest in the streets over the proposed stationing of the cruise and Pershing intermediate-range missiles worried moderate opponents of these missiles; they could not argue that the decision was unconstitutional, hence to overturn it by extraconstitutional means evoked the instability of Weimar.

European foreign policies, German included, are becoming more "American" in the degree of influence exerted by domestic politics, and American foreign policy is less "American" in this sense than Europeans often suggest: the pullings and haulings of American politics have masked considerable continuity in postwar policy toward Europe and the Soviet Union. Still, it is small wonder that Germans see American foreign policy through the lens of their own tradition as inconsistent, hostage to the passing passions of domestic politics.

Germany, an integral part of the West during the medieval period, became less so thereafter. The romanticism that influenced European culture in the first half of the nineteenth century became for Germany, in Gordon Craig's words, "that peculiarly German sense of inwardness, or remoteness from reality, of intimate community between self and the mysterious forces of nature and God."[7] Both German nationalism, under an autocratic regime with a dominant military, and its economic growth occurred with an emphasis on "a combination of inward-looking faith and outward obedience."[8] Germany became the land of *Zwischenkultur*—the culture of the "middle." No less a cosmopolitan than Max Weber spoke, on the eve of World War I, of the special mission of German culture "between Anglo-Saxon materialism and Russian barbarism."

Thus, in the trauma of Nazi defeat, the Federal Republic made a sharp break with history by identifying firmly with the West. Before, it had been *Mitteleuropa* (central Europe) in policy as well as geography. Bismarck and his successors under Weimar had pursued a *Schaukelpolitik* (seesaw policy) attempting to balance the Western nations against Russia. Bismarck's mastery was not matched by his successors, and when both ends of the seesaw, France and Russia, joined in the anti-German alliance that had been Bismarck's nightmare, the eventual result was World War I.

During Weimar, Germany was more the object of the seesaw than its manipulator. Even Rapallo was an improvisation based on the fear of an Anglo-French-Russian deal and was undertaken against the inclinations of its anti-Communist German architects. The context of the times suggests how estranged Germany was from the Western victors. The German foreign minister, Walter Rathenau, sought modest agreements with those victors that he hoped would lead to more ambitious ones until the "iron curtain"—as it was called in the 1920s, sometimes in specific reference to the demilitarized zone—between Germany and the West had fallen.

Historians will argue whether the victors or the vanquished of World War I were to blame for the sequence of events that led to Hitler and World War II. For one of the best American students of European-American relations:

> No German government [of the Weimar period] was likely to overlook the obvious facts that Poland and the other Eastern states were weak and that Germany was in a position to pursue revisionism in the East either in partnership with the Soviet Union (the Rapallo option) or with the acquiescence if not the support of the Western powers (and particularly Great Britain), perhaps in the name of defense against Bolshevism.[9]

For a German expert, by contrast:

> If history offers any lesson at all, it is that Germany has colluded with the East only when abandoned or humbled by the West. . .At Rapallo, Weimar Germany turned toward Moscow because it was treated as a pariah by the West. Thereafter, Germany's isolation provided a domestic climate where the extremes on the left and right could meet on the joint platform of an untrammeled, anti-Western nationalism that contributed to the rise of Hitler. . .[10]

Yet what should be remembered is that, whatever the cause, a balance between East and West has been traditional German policy, and so the postwar ties with the West are unusual.

Finally there is the most recent line of West German policy called *Ostpolitik*—reconciliation with its eastern neighbors. That policy began more with the Federal Republic's allies than itself. It began haltingly with President Kennedy's "strategy for peace" in the early 1960s and was confirmed more explicitly in President Johnson's "bridge building" speech of 1966 and French President Charles de Gaulle's visit to Moscow the same year. The Federal Republic's allies had decided that the way to mitigate the effects of Europe's division was to negotiate with the East, not to try to isolate it.

Once the Social Democratic Party (SPD) came to power in 1969, Chancellor Willy Brandt and Foreign Minister Walther Scheel hurried their country to the forefront of the policy of conciliation with the East

lest their allies, and especially their superpower patron, cut a deal with
the Soviet Union over their heads—one form of abandonment. They
accepted that reunification was a hope, not an operative goal, and that
the path to it lay through dealing with their eastern neighbors,
including the Soviet Union and, in particular, trying to improve the
living conditions of these neighbors, especially the German Democratic
Republic (GDR).

While that willingness to put the question of reunification in
abeyance had been foreshadowed by Adenauer in secret discussions
with Moscow as early as 1962, *Ostpolitik* as public policy marked a
break with previous efforts to isolate the GDR and limit relations with
the Soviet Union. As such, the policy was initially opposed by the
Christian Democratic Union (CDU) and its sister party, the Christian
Social Union (CSU).

Interests, Attitudes and Pressures

It has become commonplace to recognize that the Federal Republic has
specific interest—humanitarian and economic—in East-West relations
across the divide in Europe that are matched by no other ally,
especially not the United States. The 300,000 ethnic Germans who
have been allowed to emigrate from Eastern Europe and the Soviet
Union since the early 1970s are evidence of that stake; the three million
ethnic Germans who remain are reminders of how much the state of
East-West relations matters. For the Federal Republic, East-West
relations become a family affair when they involve East Germany.
Helmut Schmidt said during the 1980 crisis over the American hostages
in Iran that he sympathized with the plight of those fifty people
because he had to worry about the seventeen million East Germans
hostage to the Soviet empire.

What is less common is an appreciation of how, if at all, those
interests have changed, and the effect they have on the policies of the
Federal Republic. Certainly, the implications of those interests do not
all go in one direction. Immigrants to the Federal Republic, like those
to the United States, seldom are special pleaders for the places they
left, all the less so in the German case if the places they left were once
Germany but now are Poland or the Soviet Union. Chancellor Helmut
Kohl rediscovered that fact early in his tenure when he met with
refugee groups unreconciled to the loss of Germany's "eastern"
territories and so touched off a minor crisis in relations with the
Federal Republic's eastern neighbors.

These varied pulls on West Germans are reflected in the language they use. For many younger Germans, East Germany is both foreign and remote. Their notion of "Europe" is Western Europe and their nationalism is "little German"—the Federal Republic. They use the term "German" accordingly. Yet even for these West Germans, a larger German sense of identity breaks through, sometimes disconcertingly. Everyone has a favorite story. Mine occurred during the 1976 Olympics, when a West German colleague visited me in London. He spoke of how bad relations between the two Germanies were. But then he asked: Did you see how our girls did yesterday? "Our girls" were East German swimmers.

On balance, if relations between the two Germanies are still difficult, they are much less so than at the height of the Cold War. Since 1949, 3.2 million Germans from East Germany have emigrated west. One West German in three over age fourteen has relatives in the East, and one West German in eight visits across the border periodically; in 1987 about one million East Germans under retirement age visited the Federal Republic, twice the number of a year earlier and ten times the figure for 1985. The Federal Republic imposed economic sanctions on East Germany several times in the 1950s and 1960s; it is hard to imagine such a thing happening now.

In another area of specific interest, economics, there also has been visible change. Under Adenauer, the Federal Republic shunned trade with the East, lacking even diplomatic relations with Moscow until 1955. What trade there was with the East was conducted through a government-approved "Eastern Committee of the German Economy" (*Ostausschuss der deutschen Wirtschaft*), a kind of successor to the "Russia Committee" of the 1920s. After the beginning of *Ostpolitik*, West German trade eastward rapidly increased; trade with East Germany always had been a special case, regarded as "internal" by Bonn and so defined by its EEC partners.

Yet even now, the Federal Republic's trade with the Soviet Union and Eastern Europe (East Germany included) is not large, having declined from 5.8 percent in 1975 and 4.5 percent in 1981. It represented only a small percentage of its trade with fellow EEC members, about equaling German trade with Switzerland and amounting to only two-thirds that with the United States.

At the same time, these aggregate figures may disguise as much as they reveal. If, for example, German exports to the East are not particularly important to the overall economy, they are to specific sectors which have political clout. The pipeline disputes of 1963 and 1982 testify to these interests and their impact in the political realm.

They also illustrate an important change over time: Washington was able to impose its will on Bonn in the earlier episode but not in the later one.

After 1959 the Soviet Union became the largest single purchaser of West German steel pipe.[11] In October 1962 the three leading German producers signed a contract with the Soviet Union to sell 163,000 tons of large-diameter steel pipe in exchange for oil; the pipe was to supply the so-called Friendship Pipeline connecting the Baku oil fields to Poland, Czechoslovakia, and East Germany.

The next month the NATO Council adopted in secret an American proposal opposing the export of large-diameter pipe to the Soviet Union. Then, the main American argument was that the pipe network inside Eastern Europe and the Soviet Union might be used to supply the Soviet Army. Then, as two decades later, a major row in the Alliance ensued. The Council action was a recommendation, to be implemented at the discretion of national authorities. The Federal Republic immediately accepted the recommendation in the hope that its European partners would do the same. It also decided to apply the ban retroactively to the October deal.

In this instance, Germany was the odd man out, as Britain, France, and Italy were prepared to continue pipe exports to the Soviet Union— a fact that intensified the internal debate in Germany. The arguments were the same as those heard two decades later. Opponents of the ban argued, for instance, that it was both bad politics and bad business. They stressed, in particular, the danger of repudiating international agreements. The steel industry and labor complained bitterly that six to nine months of full-capacity work had been lost. Bundestag members from the governing CDU but with steel industry constituencies were under great pressure to toe the government line. In the end, the Adenauer government prevailed, and the ban held, but at considerable cost.

The 1982 version of the pipeline controversy is surprisingly parallel to the earlier one. This time the pipe was for natural gas, not oil, but the German companies, Mannesmann for instance, and their interests were the same. The German steel industry was second only to Japan in its dependence on exports, and it, like its competitors, had been badly hurt by the global glut of steel production capacity. In these circumstances, the importance of exports to the East for maintaining jobs and industries was far out of proportion to the aggregate figures for the economy as a whole. Between 1973 and 1979, half of German exports of large-diameter steel pipe went to the Soviet Union.[12]

At the end of December 1981, three weeks after the imposition of martial law in Poland, the United States imposed an export ban on all American parts for the pipeline and prodded the Europeans to do likewise. When they did not, six months later, immediately after the Versailles economic summit, Washington extended the sanctions to cover not only American suppliers but also their subsidiaries and license holders abroad.

The Europeans, this time including the Germans, disagreed with both the premises and the form of the action. Sanctions seemed bad in substance, since martial law was at least a *Polish* solution to the crisis in Poland, thus preferable to open Soviet intervention; moreover, the contracts already had been signed. And the "long-arm"—not to say "strong-arm"—effort by the United States to compel European subsidiaries of American firms raised the issue of extraterritoriality, an old European grievance against Washington. This time Bonn showed no sign of going along with the United States, and in the end it was Washington that relented, accepting, in November 1982, a bland European commitment to review trade policy in return for lifting its restraints.

Public attitudes as reflected in poll data are another source of evidence about what has changed and what has not. Interpreting the data is hardly a straightforward matter, but what is apparent is that broad attitudes in the Federal Republic have not changed much in nearly forty years. For nearly thirty years, German support for NATO has stayed in the 70–80 percent range, depending on how the question is asked.[13] Mikhail Gorbachev's arrival on the scene has made some difference—a spate of polls in the mid-1980s found that Germans trusted him more than they did Ronald Reagan—but it is too early to tell whether the change is an abiding one. For instance, in 1986, 35 percent of Germans in one poll reported that their view of the Soviet Union was improving, against only 17 percent in 1980, but 39 percent had so reported in 1970.[14]

There is visible change along three important dimensions. First is growing concern about nuclear weapons. In a 1980 poll, a 64–19 majority said that the Federal Republic should use "military weapons" to defend itself against attack, and a 53–31 majority was prepared to do so "even if the war is fought primarily on the soil of the Federal Republic," but only 15 percent favored defense "if nuclear weapons have to be used on the soil of the Federal Republic." Based on what evidence is available, this nuclear allergy, whose existence should not be a surprise, has increased over time. Asked to choose between avoiding war at all cost, even if it meant living under a Communist government, and defending democracy, even if it led to a nuclear war, Germans in 1955 chose the former by 36 percent to 33, with 31 undecided. By 1981, the result was 48 to 27, with 25 undecided.[15] In 1987, polls recorded Germans as being just about as enthusiastic about the prospect of eliminating U.S. and Soviet intermediate nuclear forces (INF) as other Europeans, but Germans were more likely to cite the reduced likelihood of being a target of the missiles as a reason for their enthusiasm.

Second, Germans now view the Soviet Union as less of a threat than they did several decades ago even though they now see the Soviet Union and the East as equal to or stronger than the United States and the West. In 1952 more than 80 percent of Germans viewed the Soviet Union as a threat, more than half did so in the late 1960s, but only about a third by the mid-1980s. In 1954, 40 percent thought the West stronger, 23 percent the East and 33 saw equality; by 1986, the figures were 13, 29, and 58.[16] Yet there is little straightforward relation between views of the balance and attitudes toward the Soviet Union, defense spending, or the Western alliance. Those who see the Soviet Union as superior in defense are not prone to advocate neutralism in response; quite the contrary, they are more likely to be CDU members and to express support for increased defense spending. There is, however, little support among any group for such an increase if it means lower budgets for social programs.

Third, and most intriguing, the attitudes of young Germans do differ from those of their elders, more so than is the case elsewhere in Europe. Those younger Germans, especially the better-educated ones, are more tempted by neutralism than their elders, less impressed by the United States, and less prepared to defend their countries by military means. For example, of those university-educated people over fifty sampled in a 1981 poll, well before any Gorbachev effect, only 5 percent favored neutrality over NATO; among similarly-educated 18–34 year olds, however, that percentage rose to 28.[17] It is precisely these better-educated, younger Germans that have been the constituency for the Greens.

Exactly why this difference exists is a matter for speculation, but certainly the experience of the different German generations has varied considerably.[18] Not only are the young unfamiliar with the dark days of the early postwar period that called forth American beneficence in the form of the Marshall Plan, the American connection through NATO, and that justified Germany's dependence, many of them came of age during the Vietnam War, and their image of America is sharply different from that of their elders. Perhaps, by contrast, older French people were less likely to idealize the United States early in the postwar period and so less prone to disillusionment later. The experience of the British has been more continuous than those of their continental counterparts—neither the trauma of defeat nor the vigor of reconstruction, and continuity in both relative affinity for the United States and in postwar economic decline.[19]

No doubt the differences will mute with time; as the younger Germans age, they will move toward more orthodox positions. Yet it seems likely that some differences will remain: across the political spectrum, younger Germans moving into leadership roles will be more skeptical of the United States, more assertive in dealing with Washington, and more nationalistic in their insistence that German interests be recognized by their allies. The Bitburg cemetery episode illustrated these changes; most Germans did not want to forget the Holocaust, but rather they wanted to be treated like other nations in honoring their dead-in-arms.

The Emerging German Consensus

These days, when the Americans or the French fret about trends in the Federal Republic, they most often bemoan the breakup of that country's internal consensus on security issues, noting in particular that the CDU and its allies supported the deployment of Pershings and cruise missiles in Germany while the SPD drifted into opposition to it after 1983. The consensus, however, never was as complete as we now remember, nor is the disintegration as great as we now fear. In one light, the *Ostpolitik* of Brandt and Scheel and then the embrace of it by the CDU in the 1970s represented a kind of return to the historic pattern of German relations that sought a balance between East and West. In another, though, that consensus around *Ostpolitik* stood in contrast to both the policy and the controversy that had preceded it.

Now, the broad middle ground of West Germany policy has moved, a fact at least as striking as the apparent disintegration of consensus. There seems to be emerging a rough agreement among the main political forces except the Greens.

That consensus is as follows:

- The primacy of German stakes in a stable Europe is accepted by all.
- Thus trade and humanitarian contacts across the East-West divide in Europe are a good thing in any season. Economic sanctions, for any purpose, are correspondingly bad.

- Arms control is similarly good almost irrespective of agreements. More is better.
- Given the minimal threat of Soviet aggression against Western Europe, nuclear deterrence is a fact and will continue with many fewer nuclear weapons based in Germany.
- In the interest of stability in Europe, the Federal Republic should detach itself politically from the United States in areas beyond Europe.

This emerging German consensus is not all new, but it does reflect both the embrace of the SPD's position by the CDU and the seeping into mainstream politics of the antinuclear allergy reflected in opinion polls. On the Federal Republic's relations with the East, a CDU leader has said:

> Because of our geographic situation and because of our history, we Germans are obligated to maintain good relations with West and East. For us Germans there are many historical ties to the East. We share a deep understanding of the cultural unity of Europe, in all its variety and with all its differences.[20]

The words are Helmut Kohl's, but they might have been Helmut Schmidt's. Schmidt's own conversion—from a politician whose ties were all with the West to a chancellor who spoke often and passionately about the Federal Republic's links eastward—was something of a surprise.

Even more surprising, though, was how quickly and completely the CDU/CSU government made the same policies, and even the same language, its own, just as it had adopted *Ostpolitik* and the Eastern treaties after opposing them a decade earlier. In 1983 it made a fresh loan of over a billion DM to East Germany, a loan, moreover, negotiated by Franz-Josef Strauss, the CSU leader and fervent anti-Communist. In deciding to deal with the division of Germany through ties with the East, the Federal Republic acquired an interest in détente almost no matter what. It also accepted Soviet leverage, through East Germany, not over the Federal Republic's internal arrangements but over its foreign policy.

Party politics are not irrelevant, however. The CDU government explicitly stated that the German question was still open, while, by contrast, the Free Democrats are careful to style themselves as the party of negotiation within the coalition government, a trend accentuated by Foreign Minister Hans-Dietrich Genscher's personal stake in his image as the steady hand on foreign policy in both social democratic and conservative governments. Yet the consensus across the parties is at least as prominent as the differences among them.

The last plank of the consensus—detachment from the United States beyond Europe—is new mainly in that it is now more explicit. In the 1950s and 1960s it was taken for granted that Germany had nothing to contribute beyond Europe but rhetorical solidarity. Not so now, and so the German interest in decoupling has been more and more visible. In the aftermath of the Soviet invasion of Afghanistan in 1979, for example, German and other European officials constantly echoed the view that the Soviet invasion was a grave matter, and the West had to react strongly. Yet, another view was evident. In that view, Afghanistan mattered but did not change the basic East-West balance. Soviet weaknesses remained. Besides, the invasion owed something to Western policy, to signals of disinterest in the fate of Afghanistan after the April 1978 coup and to America's inability to provide much by way of positive incentives for Soviet restraint in Soviet-American détente, for instance by getting SALT II ratified. This view also stressed the German interest in protecting European détente even in a time of superpower tension, an obvious reflection of the different stakes between Europe and America. The West, it was said, should not be the first to import tension into Europe from outside it.[21]

The ragged edges of the emerging consensus were apparent in the German debate during 1987 over the zero-zero option—bans on Soviet and American long-range and short-range intermediate nuclear forces (INF). The idea was hard to resist: public opinion was for it, and, after all, the single-zero option (a ban on long-range INF) originally was an American idea embraced by the Allies.

Yet the strategic logic of double-zero was troubling to many Alliance-minded Germans. It left in place the least palatable of land-based nuclear weapons, artillery and missiles with ranges so short they could only explode on German territory, and so guaranteed public pressure to remove those short-range weapons. That, in turn, raised the specter of "denuclearization," thus threatening the nuclear connection between the Federal Republic and the United States on which deterrence has been assumed to depend.

The substantive debate was reflected in intracoalition politics: Genscher favored zero-zero, while others in the coalition, especially in the defense ministry, were reluctant. In the end, the Kohl government moved, grudgingly, to embrace zero-zero. It resisted, then relented on, including the ninety-six Pershing I missiles in Germany under dual-key—that is, with launchers owned by German forces but warheads under American control.

A Decoupling Federal Republic in a Not-Yet Decoupled Europe?[22]

A straight-line projection of the trends outlined in this chapter would imply increasing distance between German and American attitudes toward the Soviet Union and correspondingly increased chances for strain in German-American relations. Germans will continue to feel a natural vocation to the East; even if economic interchange remains relatively small, the economies of Eastern Europe will continue to be complementary to that of the Federal Republic. The broad view of the Soviet Union-as-threat will be different in the Federal Republic from that in the United States, perhaps most different among the cohort of people now in their forties and so on the verge of national political power.

The Germans of that group will remain supporters of the alliance with the United States—only the Greens oppose that alliance and some of them do so in the context of both blocs in Europe dissolving—but that support will be more grudging and conditional. It will be grudging because of the lack of alternatives and the dependence enshrined in the status quo, and conditional on having space to pursue German interests, including in relations with the Soviet Union, even when these do not coincide with American interests.[23]

If West Germans remain attached to the Alliance, this Alliance will be different. It will be one in which it is no longer an article of faith that, in the end, the United States must be given its way, an Alliance in which consultations must take due account of specifically German interests. That pattern of consultations seems likely, moreover, to be characterized more often by the table-thumping that was characteristic of German diplomacy before the shame of the Third Reich imposed a guilty deference.[24] (In that regard, Helmut Kohl is a throwback. A better guide to the future is Helmut Schmidt, a man who not only thought he should be president of the United States but who seems, for a time during the Ford administration, to have thought he was— behaving with considerable incaution, even if he never actually thumped the table.)

When, in 1984, Senator Sam Nunn introduced an amendment requiring the European NATO allies to meet certain force goals or face the prospect of American troop withdrawals, the reaction of Karsten Voigt, a former Young Socialist leader and now a foreign affairs spokesman in the Bundestag, exemplified this change in attitude: "We're no banana republic!" Nunn is hardly an enemy of NATO, and Voigt knew that the senator's amendment was, in tactical terms, friendly, intended to head off pressures for something worse. Yet it rankled: who was Nunn, a single American senator, to tell the Europeans what they should do?

The strain seems likely to be all the worse because American support for NATO, too, is becoming more conditional, and the American conditions mirror the German ones. Isolationism is all but dead in the United States—of the presidential candidates in 1988, Rev. Jesse Jackson came closest to fitting that label in his desire to define U.S. interests in the world very narrowly and concentrate on problems at home. Yet across the political spectrum hand-wringing about the U.S. economy has brought forth another round, modest thus far, of concern over "burden-sharing"—the feeling that the United States does too much in the common defense while Europe (and Japan) do too little.[25]

Moreover, isolationism's near kin, unilateralism, is not dead. It has lurked beneath the surface of the American foreign policy debate, partly reflecting nostalgia for images of past American strength but partly also reflecting impatience with allies and friends. Unilateralist impulses, too, are spread across the political spectrum but are most powerful on the right. They are present among neoconservatives like Irving Kristol who would condition American support for the defense of Europe on tougher European policies toward the Soviet Union; among those, like Senator Ted Stevens of Alaska, who are tempted to scale down American forces in Europe to build them up for contingencies in the Persian Gulf; and even among staunch defenders of NATO like Senator Nunn, who nevertheless feel that the U.S. bears too much of the burden.[26]

In the United States, as in Germany, the Alliance is at best a matter of necessity; it no longer fires the imaginations of statesmen or politicians as it once did. It is to be supported just as far as it meets American interests and no further—again, no sea-change but a gradual evolution. Moreover, the conditions under which a broad spectrum of Americans would support it are in a way the opposite of likely German attitudes: those Americans would agree it merited support if it proved a reliable way of recruiting European support for American policies. (Indeed, given Americans' persistent sense of loneliness in the world, what the Allies say is almost more important than what they do: witness strong French support for deploying the Pershings and cruise missiles, although France itself had no thought of taking any.)

Some of the issues of strain are predictable. In embracing zero-zero provided it is the end of nuclear arms control in Europe, the Reagan administration has bequeathed its successor a puzzler; once zero-zero is agreed, even German conservatives will find it hard to resist Soviet calls and their own public pressure for negotiations to reduce battlefield nuclear weapons: after all, why should NATO retain only those nuclear weapons that can only destroy German territory? German consensus on that point will, however, appear craven to Americans. Or, American governments will propose a nuclear modernization in Europe, for instance of Lance short-range missiles, which will be broadly unacceptable in the Federal Republic, at least once voters learn of it.

Another consequence of zero-zero will be renewed attention to the conventional balance of forces in Europe. In the short run Germans and Americans alike, across the political spectrum, will proclaim the need for conventional arms control. Yet familiar differences already are visible on this issue and are likely to sharpen over time. For instance, Americans will argue that nuclear reductions call for conventional improvements as well as arms control, and may be tempted by a conventional version of the INF dual track—force improvements as an inducement to arms control.

Given the different views of the conventional balance, Americans will reckon the prospects of arms control dimmer than Germans, seeing little reason for the Soviet Union to relinquish the advantages provided by its conventional preponderance in Europe. Germans, by contrast, will take Gorbachev's encouraging hints as indications that the Soviet leader has his own economic reasons for wanting to remove some Soviet forces from Eastern Europe. Americans will say that only very asymmetrical reductions—five or more for the Warsaw Pact to one for NATO—can improve the military balance in Europe, while Germans will be prepared to settle for less.

More generally, the German-American fault-line over how to deal with Moscow will become more visible, Americans emphasizing Western solidarity and tenacity, Germans flexibility and negotiation. Whether Gorbachev appears to be succeeding or failing internally, Americans are likely to argue that firmness serves the West's purposes. Germans may say nearly the opposite, that in either case Gorbachev should be helped.

Strain over issues outside Europe is also predictable. The ingredients for trans-Atlantic division are all there: Germans will want to decouple from American policy, even in the Persian Gulf, so as not to introduce regional tension into Europe; but Americans will assert that those regional interests, like oil, are more important to Europe than to America; Germany will argue that it is especially constrained by its constitution and its NATO commitment; and while for issues *inside* Europe there is sometimes a degree of American deference to European views since, after all, it is *their* continent, there will be no such deference beyond Europe.

The Reagan administration did not press the Federal Republic to move forces into the Gulf in 1987–1988, but the chances of a dispute that will erupt under the pressure of events will remain. Suppose tightening oil markets in the 1990s give the Gulf a salience it did not have in the 1980s despite the Iran-Iraq war. At a minimum, an "unfair" sharing of the burden outside Europe will be part of the litany of complaints in any American political backlash against the Alliance.

The Soviet Union and More Dramatic Change

These assessments have assumed considerable continuity in Soviet policy. On that assumption, they amount to more of the same for German governments that are attached to good relations with the East and more than faintly Gaullist[27] in their dealings with Washington. But what, then, might conduce to dramatic change in the Federal Republic's position? Two related questions are worth considering: one is the attractiveness of alternatives to current dependence on the United States, in the context of changing perceptions of the Soviet Union; the other is Soviet policy more directly.

For the last several decades, Germany's status in the Alliance has persisted less because of its inherent attractiveness than for want of alternatives: going it alone or going East has seemed either too expensive or too unsettling or both—to both Germans and neighbors; conventional defense has been regarded as both expensive and bad in principle; a nuclear Germany has been ruled out; and there has been no "Europe" with which to cooperate in the security realm.

If Germans cannot be tolerably confident that the United States' nuclear commitment to them is credible, despite the huge American arsenal, why, for example, should they trust the much smaller, and more "national" French or British nuclear forces? Moreover, the idea of dependence on France is no more attractive than dependence on America, at least for most Germans. In that sense Helmut Schmidt's 1984 proposal for far-reaching Franco-German cooperation was surprisingly anachronistic in its willingness to trade German money for French nuclear protection.

Yet suppose, for example, that German's sense of threat from the Soviet Union continues to attenuate. With each passing year that seems likely almost no matter what the course of Soviet force improvements in Eastern Europe. With Gorbachev and his adroit diplomacy as the principal new contextual factor, the threat seems likely to diminish all the more rapidly. Then, with the need to buy insurance declining, Germans might become less finicky about the insurer. Some form of French (or even British) nuclear pledge might be enough, coupled with some sleight of hand about Franco-German consultation in nuclear targeting and, perhaps, whatever remained of the American commitment. In those circumstances, the Federal Republic might move quite far toward denuclearization; American nuclear weapons, save perhaps aircraft-delivered ones, might be withdrawn from the European land mass.

These developments, none probable and all gradual, would produce change in the trans-Atlantic relationship from *within* the Alliance: if Germany decided it needed less nuclear protection from the United States, that would set in motion a process leading to less American commitments of all sorts, and the Alliance would be thus transformed.

The second alternative to dependence is a nuclear Federal Republic, either on its own or as the senior partner in a nuclear Western Europe. On that score, General de Gaulle's strategic logic was impeccable, though he was careful not to carry it to its logical conclusion: if Europe—and Germany—fear that America will not push the button, then they need buttons of their own with nuclear weapons to match. For Germany to be serious about defense and seriously independent, half-way measures of association with Britain or France will not do. That is true even though geography limits the extent to which France can be decoupled from Germany.

The idea of a nuclear Federal Republic strains the imagination. No Germans are flirting with the idea now, although some were doing so three decades ago when there was less need as we now perceive it.[28] Yet a nuclear Germany seems to me the *strategic* track we are on.[29] To be sure, that is strategic not *political* logic. What the first suggests, the second seems to rule out. And to be credible, a German nuclear force would have to be more variegated than existing British or French forces lest it be beset by credibility problems of its own; Britain and France are not threatened by limited or half-accidental wars, thus their threats to use strategic weapons if the war comes to them are tolerably credible. In turn, however, the need for a varied German force would make the political obstacles to building it, within and outside the Federal Republic, all the more formidable.

It also strains the imagination to see how such a force might come about. The United States might come to favor a nuclear Germany in a world of denuclearization beyond zero-zero and sharp constraints on defense budgets. Or American actions might promote it without meaning to: suppose an economic collapse plus other disputes estranged the United States and the Federal Republic. Surely, however, an incipient German nuclear force would set off alarm bells in Moscow. Yet the Soviet Union might be unable to prevent such a force: suppose estrangement within the Western Alliance combined with a menacing turn in Soviet policy.

In these circumstances, improbable if not impossible, a German government might find nuclear weapons a means of minimal deterrence on the cheap, which would be all the more attractive if the bulk of those weapons were strategic and thus based at sea, not on land. Stretching the speculation still further, the nuclear option would, it seems to me, be more appealing to a German government of the left than of the right, one that would be nationalist but primarily interested in social spending, hence unwilling to build a serious conventional defense.[30] To be sure, such a government would have first to control the nuclear allergy that is so much in evidence at present.

A final possibility, dramatic change in Soviet policy, is on its face about as unlikely as a nuclear Federal Republic, for it would mean contemplating a new postwar order in Europe. That order serves Europe well by dividing German power, and so solving the problem with which the continent grappled unsuccessfully for seventy years. It also serves the United States by ratifying the American presence in Europe. The status quo seems to serve the Soviet Union at least as well. By dividing Germany, it diminishes the German threat; by dividing the continent as well as Germany it gives the Soviet Union leverage over the Federal Republic, justifies a large Soviet military presence in Eastern Europe, and provides some legitimacy for regimes in Eastern Europe that lack the usual sources of it.

Why should even Gorbachev take the risk of changing that happy state of affairs? His predecessors toyed with the idea of a neutralized, demilitarized Germany or, more fleetingly, with some kind of special relationship with the Federal Republic.[31] This ceased in the mid-1950s, and Moscow shifted toward at least acceptance of a permanently divided Germany, preferably with some military limitations on the western part. By 1970 or so Soviet leaders seem to have settled on a combination of a tight hold on East Germany and limited détente with the Federal Republic. They have tried to loosen the Federal Republic's ties to the West without having to come near the question of whether they would like actually to succeed at that task.

Even while he was flirting with reunification, Khrushchev told Guy Mollet in 1956 that he preferred 17 million Germans on his side to 70 million in a neutral and reunited Germany. Gorbachev, too, is likely to reach a similar conclusion and so to limit his ambition to more adroit diplomacy in pursuit of what has become orthodox policy. Nor is neutralism part of the German tradition; Germany has always been too big to be neutral. Neutralism-for-reunification was, for the SPD in the

1950s, more a hope than a policy, and it was rejected in 1960 when the party became serious about governing.

Yet these verities might not be eternal. As Gorbachev confronts *his* problems, he might convince his Politburo colleagues to take unprecedented risks.[32] American actions seem likely to affect these Soviet calculations only indirectly, through their effects on German policy. Dramatic change in Soviet policy toward Germany might result from internal developments. In the past, foreign policy shifts have followed from Soviet domestic politics: witness Soviet acceptance of Romania's limited independence and of the Austrian State Treaty, both of which owed something to intraparty maneuvering in the wake of Stalin's death. Gorbachev and his colleagues might, for instance, come to believe the Soviet economy required a massive military withdrawal from Eastern Europe; or that domestic reform required different responses, even different regimes from Eastern Europe.

History suggests that Eastern Europe, especially East Germany, is another critical part of the problem as perceived by Gorbachev.[33] If the Federal Republic is important in Soviet calculations, East Germany is even more so. The GDR accounts for a tenth of all Soviet trade and is the major supplier of industrial goods, in part because technology seeps easily to the East through intra-German trade. When the Soviet Union opted for more trade with the Federal Republic in the early 1970s, it finally had to engineer the replacement of East German leader Ulbricht, a man of stature in Moscow, the last surviving of Lenin's colleagues.

Since the deployment of the missiles in 1983, the Soviet Union has watched warily as the two Germanies have sought to insulate their relations from superpower tension and succeeded in achieving a measure of such insulation. A continuation of that intra-German détente might push the Soviet Union to try to crack down, or induce it to contemplate new policies, or both. Or events might reconfigure Moscow's German problem: who would have thought two decades ago that pan-German sentiments would be more alive in the East than the West, complete with a bizarre celebration of Luther's birthday?

If the *means* of West German policy, *Ostpolitik*, make the Federal Republic the champion of stability in the short run, the long-term *goal* of that policy is to erode the existing order. West Germans are the biggest Western losers from the postwar order in Europe, and so have the most to gain from its modification. It is intriguing to note that the Greens have been much more vocal about human rights in the East than has the SPD, and thus in their own way more upsetting to the existing order.

Is it now unthinkable that several decades hence the reunifiers in the East might be joined by those now-young West Germans who find it hard to choose between the materialism and nuclear weapons on their side of the Wall and the closed society on the other side?[34] While neutralism in pursuit of pan-Germanism has tempted only fringe groups in German politics for three decades—now it is the Greens who sometimes evoke the vision—public opinion polls record surprising interest in the idea. When Allensbach polls asked whether West Germans would welcome a nonaligned, unified Germany free to decide its own social political system, 42 percent said they welcomed the idea in 1986, an increase from 38 percent in 1978.[38]

So far it seems safe to assume that these poll results reflect, much like SPD policy in the 1950s, a desire to escape from growing East-West tension rather than a current policy preference; few of those in the polls who favored the idea thought it feasible. Yet suppose that Soviet policy changing under the pressure of events made it so?

Notes

1. Terminology is always a problem when writing about Germany. I use "German" or "Germany" to refer to pre-1945 events; when used in reference to post-1945 events, they mean either the broad German nation or, in shorthand, the Federal Republic. East Germany or the German Democratic Republic (GDR) are explicitly labeled as such.
2. For more detailed argument and evidence on this point, see chapter 2 of my *Making the Alliance Work: The United States and Western Europe* (Ithaca, NY: Cornell University Press, 1985).
3. Many commentators have used variants of this language. See, in particular, Michael Mandelbaum, *The Nuclear Revolution: International Politics Before and After Hiroshima* (Cambridge: Cambridge University Press, 1981), pp. 151–153; and Glenn Snyder, "The Security Dilemma in Alliance Politics," *World Politics*, 36, 4 (1984), 461–493.
4. This is a point that I came to appreciate from my friend and former colleague, Christoph Bertram. See his "European Security and the German Problem," *International Security*, 4 (Winter 1979–1980).
5. Ralf Dahrendorf, "The Europeanization of Europe," in Andrew J. Pierre, ed., *A Widening Atlantic? Domestic Change and Foreign Policy* (New York: Council on Foreign Relations, 1986), p. 32.
6. Quoted in Gordon A. Craig, *From Bismarck to Adenauer: Aspects of German Statecraft* (Baltimore: The Johns Hopkins Press, 1958), p. 18.
7. *The Germans* (New York: G.P. Putnam's Sons, 1982), p. 190.
8. Richard Loewenthal, "Cultural Change and Generation Change in Postwar West Germany," in James A. Cooney and others, *The Federal Republic of Germany and the United States: Changing Political, Social and Economic Relations*, (Boulder, Co: Westview Press, 1984), p. 34. The Weber quote is from *ibid.*, p. 35.

9. Anton de Porte, *Europe Between the Superpowers: The Enduring Balance* (New Haven: Yale University Press, 1979), p. 33.

10. Josef Joffe, "All Quiet on the Eastern Front," *Foreign Policy*, 37 (Winter 1979–1980), p. 163.

11. Good sources on this episode, similar in most particulars, are Angela Stent, *From Embargo to Ostpolitik: The Political Economy of West German-Soviet Relations, 1955–1980* (Cambridge: Cambridge University Press, 1981), p. 91ff; and Robert W. Dean, *West German Trade with the East: The Political Dimension* (New York: Praeger, 1974).

12. Angela E. Stent, *Soviet Energy and Eastern Europe*, Washington Papers 90 (Washington: CSIS, 1982), p. 24.

13. See Allensbach polls, cited in Hans Peter Schwarz, "The West Germans, Western Democracy, and Western Ties in Light of Public Opinion Research," in Cooney and others, p. 67. ENMID polls record the same results. For instance, in 1966, 63 percent of respondents favored staying in NATO in its present form, 3 percent were for withdrawing; in 1986 the percentages were 75 and 8, respectively. As reported in *Bundeswehr Aktuell*, October 29, 1986.

14. One prominent Reagan-Gorbachev poll was reported in *Welt am Sonntag*, May 10, 1987; on the Soviet image, see the ENMID poll cited above.

15. Kenneth Adler and Douglas Wertman, "Is NATO in Trouble?: A Survey of European Attitudes," *Public Opinion* (August/September 1981), pp. 10–11.

16. For the data on threat, see Hans Rattinger, "The Federal Republic of Germany: Much Ado about (Almost) Nothing," in Gregory Flynn and Hans Rattinger, eds., *The Public and Atlantic Defense* (Paris: Atlantic Institute for International Affairs) p. 19; on the relative balance, see ENMID polls, cited in Schwarz, p. 87, and *Welt am Sonntag*, cited above.

17. Cited in Stephen F. Szabo, ed., *The Successor Generation: International Perspectives of Postwar Europeans* (London: Butterworths, 1983), p. 172.

18. For a summary of arguments and evidence, see Harald Mueller and Thomas Risse-Kappen, "Origins of Estrangement: The Peace Movement and the Changed Image of America in West Germany," *International Security*, 12, 1 (Summer 1987).

19. *Ibid.*

20. Quoted in Gebhard Schweigler, "Domestic Setting of West German Foreign Policy," in Uwe Nerlich and James A. Thomson, eds., *The Soviet Problem in American-German Relations* (New York: Crane Russak, 1985), p. 44.

21. See, for example, the articles by Theo Sommer in *Die Zeit*, February 22 and 29, and June 27, 1980.

22. The echo of Fritz Stern is intentional. See his "Germany in a Semi-Gaullist Europe," *Foreign Affairs*, 58, 4 (Spring 1980), 867–886.

23. The themes in this and the following few paragraphs are central to my *Making the Alliance Work*, cited above. See, especially, chapters 3 and 6.

24. Even during Weimar, President Paul von Hindenburg complained of his foreign minister, Stresemann, that he did not pound the table often enough. Gordon Craig, "Germany and the United States: Some Historical Parallels and Differences and their Reflection in Attitudes toward Foreign Policy," in Cooney and others, p. 27.

25. This is the central thesis of David Calleo's *Beyond American Hegemony: The Future of the Western Alliance* (New York: Basic Books, 1987).

26. In October 1982, for instance, the Senate Appropriations Committee, at the behest of Senator Stevens' subcommittee on defense, called for a cap on the number of U.S. forces in Europe. It also reported that it was "greatly disturbed that the U.S. commitment to European security in terms of force levels and defense expenditures continues to escalate while our NATO allies' share of defense steadily declines." Reported in *Congressional Quarterly*, October 9, 1982, p. 2650. For a selection of neoconservative views on the alliance, see Irving Kristol, "What's Wrong with NATO?" *New York Times Magazine*, September 15, 1983; Norman Podhoretz, "The Present Danger," *Commentary*, March 1980; and Walter Laqueur, "Euro-Neutralism," *Commentary*, June 1980.

27. "Gaullist" is misused in Alliance affairs at least as much as "Finlandization." Here I intend it to denote nationalism and independence from the United States, the opposite of "Atlanticist," not to refer more specifically to any of the good general's notions of Europe's future.

28. Some other analysts of Europe were so flirting in the 1980s, however. See, for instance, the late Hedley Bull's, "European Self-Reliance and the Reform of NATO," *Foreign Affairs*, 61, 4 (Spring 1983), 874–892.

29. I spell out why in my "Change and Continuity in the Atlantic Alliance: The Strategic Realm," forthcoming. Conversations with Philip Bobbitt have sharpened my thinking on that issue. See his *Democracy and Deterrence* (New York: Oxford University Press, 1987).

30. If this seems far-fetched, I do have some company. See Mueller and Risse-Kappen, cited above.

31. Konrad Adenauer reports on Khrushchev's approach with regard to the latter in his *Erinnerungen* (Stuttgart, 1966), p. 528, as cited in Ernest R. May, "Soviet Policy and 'the German Problem,'" *Naval War College Review* (September-October 1983), p. 26.

32. The following discussion owes much to *ibid*.

33. See Hannes Adomeit, "The German Factor in Soviet *Westpolitik*," *Annals of the American Academy*, 481 (September 1985), pp. 15–28.

34. For a somewhat overdrawn but interesting analysis of the antinuclear movement in West Germany and its broader implications for society, see Clay Clemens, "The Antinuclear Movement in West Germany: *Angst* and Isms, Old and New," in James E. Dougherty and Robert L. Pfaltzgraff, Jr., *Shattering Europe's Defense Consensus: The Antinuclear Protest Movement and the Future of NATO* (Washington: Pergamon-Brassey's, 1985).

35. Cited in Schwarz, p. 79.

France and the Soviet Union

Pierre Hassner

At least since de Gaulle, France has often been seen by its allies, and has liked to see itself, as the maverick country, more interested in showing its independence than in reaching a consensus. Is this true for its policies toward the Soviet Union? If so, is the cause to be found in the specifics of the Franco-Soviet relationship or in the general character of French foreign policy? Is the result a difference in substance compared with the policies of other Western powers or only of method and style? If the constraints of international politics are such that all Western powers have, sooner or later, to travel along the same path, are the French, more often than not, out of step because they are ahead of the pack or because they trail behind it? And if both are true, is this because the French, as has been said of de Gaulle, live more in the world of the day before yesterday and the day after tomorrow than in the present one? Or rather because they follow a steadier course, avoiding, in particular, the fluctuations of their American allies? Or because they try to exercise a kind of countercyclical influence, balancing or moderating the fashions of the day? Or are the French different, finally, because, if they have to act like everyone else, at least they want to do it at times and places of their own choosing?

These are the questions this chapter will try to discuss. The tentative answers proposed are:

1. The basic factors to which French policy has had to respond have been, of course, on the one hand, the Soviet Union's position as one of the two superpowers and as a potential candidate for continental hegemony, and on the other, the Communist character of its regime. But France's reactions are strongly influenced by a number of features of its own situation and tradition.

First, given its geographical situation, it is neither directly dominated nor directly threatened by the Soviet Union. Rather, France sees its relations with the Soviet Union as one side in a series of triangular relations, with Germany as the traditional immediate and potential threat, the United States, as the hegemonic leader of the coalition of which willy-nilly France is a member, and, to a lesser extent, Eastern Europe, particularly Poland to the extent Paris feels morally, ideologically, or diplomatically obliged to protect its independence.

Second, France's colonial empire in the past and, today, the attempt to continue playing an extra-European role, have brought it (particularly during the Indochina war and the Suez crisis) into conflict with the Soviet Union.

Third, France's own independent nuclear deterrent and the freedom to develop it has become a central element in French foreign policy. This has led France until recently, to see arms control more as a threat than as a hope (except in the case of the ABM treaty) and to be particularly distrustful of Soviet plans for denuclearizing Europe or abolishing nuclear weapons altogether.

Fourth, France has a large Communist party: even in the Assembly elected in 1986, when the party had considerably declined, a left-wing majority was impossible without it. This has had an influence on French policy toward the Soviet Union, particularly since the formation of the Union of the left in 1972. This influence has sometimes been straightforward, with the socialists in opposition moderating their criticism of the Soviet Union in order not to jeopardize their alliance with the Communists (the PCF) while the Gaullist or conservative governments in turn would emphasize the evils of the Soviet Union in order to discredit the left. But more often and more interestingly the tables have been turned: the conservative governments have been eager for good relations with the Soviet Union, in the hope that Moscow would use its influence on the French Communist party to prevent the left from coming to power; conversely, François Mitterrand, having brought the Communists into his government, was all the more inclined during his first years in office to take a hard line toward the Soviet Union since he had to show French voters and his Western allies that he was not a prisoner of the PCF.

A fifth factor that has contributed to the originality of the French position is the peculiar role of the country's intellectuals. Of course France, as the country of reason of state, has been rather less influenced in its foreign policies by public moods and social movements than other democracies. The Fourth and the Fifth Republics have been accustomed to the opposition of the intelligentsia dominated by the left wing. During two periods, however, intellectuals both affected and reflected the public mood to such an extent that they influenced policy. This was the case just after the end of World War II, when the role of the Communists in the French resistance and that of the Red Army in the victory against nazism created a favorable disposition toward the Soviet Union, which acted as a bridge between de Gaulle and revolutionary intellectuals. It happened again, with the opposite effect, in the late 1970s and early 1980s when Solzhenitsyn's enormous success and the French left-wing intellectuals' abandonment of the cult of the Soviet Union and of more romantic revolutions produced a very strong mood hostile to Moscow and supportive of human rights, Soviet dissidents, and Polish Solidarity. Again Mitterrand, who had his own political and strategic reasons to harden France's stance toward the Soviet Union, used this mood for a time at least in his declaratory policies. The reawakening of the human rights and universalistic dimension of French foreign policy do create a constraint on France's relations with the East.

The last factor that sets France apart from its allies and that may be the most important is de Gaulle himself. It is through his person that almost all the others, and certainly those linked to France's diplomatic tradition and strategic ambitions, have had their impact. In a way the history of the variations of French policy on East-West relations since World War II is the history of the fight between, on the one hand, de Gaulle's partly anachronistic, partly prophetic vision and projection for France and for Europe and, on the other hand, the resistance to them of the international environment.

2. The result of these singular factors is that several times since 1945, France has tried to go its own way in relations with the Soviet Union, only to have to retreat to the common Western position. This happened twice with de Gaulle. His policy in the immediate postwar period and that of his immediate successors like Georges Bidault was based on the idea of a third force and of a special Franco-Russian alliance against the German danger until the reality of the Cold War forced its abandonment after 1947–1948. De Gaulle tried a modified version of the same policy again in 1965 to 1968. Again events, in particular the Soviet invasion of Prague, forced him and his successors to retreat after 1968—while waging a largely rhetorical rearguard battle against the division of Europe into two opposed blocs.

Now, however, history has taken a new twist: with a certain delay, other countries, notably the Federal Republic and the United States, have resumed the Gaullist path of détente and bilateral relations with the Soviet Union. This time it is France that is sternly reminding its allies of the necessity of maintaining a military balance, of the dangers of decoupling Europe from the United States, and of the nature of the Soviet regime. This is partly due to long-standing fears of "a new

Yalta" or "a new Rapallo," to the fact that the new Soviet-American détente is centered on arms control, to the recent questioning of the role of nuclear weapons in Western defense policy, and to the renewed French attention to the problem of human rights.

However, since 1984, President Mitterrand has shown concern at the prospect of France being the last true believer in the Cold War and of being cut off from the emerging détente. French public opinion, while less impressed by Gorbachev than the rest of Europe, is not immune to his appeal. Once more, France is moving toward the Western mainstream in order not to lose leverage on its allies, but only in a way that does not compromise its own diplomatic and strategic independence, particularly in nuclear matters.

3. The French attitude toward the Alliance is paradoxical. For France, allied unity is not a value in itself. On the contrary, the Gaullist tradition is still strong enough to ensure that, even when it objectively converges or actually cooperates with its allies, France has to be seen to be doing so for its own reasons and in its own way. On the other hand, nobody is more alert than the French (particularly the French Gaullists) to the dangers of German or American Gaullism. Hence the one incentive for French backing of a united Western or European policy toward the Soviet Union is the specter of German neutralism and American unilateralism.

The Background: Structure and History

Actual French policies toward the Soviet Union have been the result of specific combinations of the various influences—from the structural to the personal, from the domestic to the geographic—that have shaped them. In each period almost all factors have come into play, but in such diverse proportions and combinations as to produce widely contrasting results.

There are, it should be noted, two extreme but widespread beliefs: One is that French policy toward the Soviet Union has been essentially erratic, based primarily upon the whims, resentments, and fantasies of its leaders. The other holds that the policy has been based on the permanent and inalienable national interests of France, obviously and objectively determined by its geographic situation and its historical mission.

These two simple views (that one could call pure anti-Gaullist and pure Gaullist) have one common feature: the weakness of direct Franco-Soviet relations.

Between the two countries there are no common borders, no conflicts of territory or of minorities, no military confrontation or shared responsibility for world peace.

At the level of popular feelings and perceptions, one does not find the love-hate relationship and the mutual fascination that characterize Soviet-German relations. On the Soviet side this is obvious. But the French public has never been truly enthusiastic about Russia, either, except during two short periods: that of the Franco-Russian alliance in the early 1890s when a real "Russian craze" swept over France, and that of the end of World War II when the heroism of the Red Army and the sufferings of the Russian people at the hands of the Germans produced a wave of sympathy all over the West. In both cases, the events of 1917 and 1947 put an end to the love affair and replaced it (abruptly in the first case, more slowly and moderately in the second) with a prevailing hostility toward the Communist regime mixed with contempt for Russian backwardness.[1]

In neither case, however, were these negative feelings dominated by racial hatred or nationalist stereotypes. Rather, the lack of intense feelings as well as immediate interests has left the field to more abstract, indirect global factors: ideology and *Realpolitik*. These are the two great forces that have most influenced French policy toward Russia and, then, the Soviet Union.

This was already the case in the nineteenth century. Even before communism, the ideological element was present. To many French observers, the best known of whom is the Marquis de Custine, Russia was both a mysterious, closed, alien, and despotic society and a threat to the peace of Europe; as Custine put it, "the slave on his knees dreams of world empire." The historian Jules Michelet could write: "Russia does not accept from us anything but evil. It absorbs into itself all the poison of Europe. It gives it back increased and more dangerous. Yesterday, it was telling us: 'I am Christianity,' tomorrow it will tell us: 'I am socialism.'"[2]

These perceptions became a political force through the Russian repression of national revolts in East Central Europe, particularly in Poland, and the persecution of the Jews. In 1831, La Fayette could exclaim: "The whole of France is Polish!" In 1867, the young lawyer Charles Floquet verbally attacked the Czar who was visiting Paris with the famous, "*Vive la Pologne, Monsieur!*"

Of course, there was a domestic dimension to these campaigns. By attacking France's monarchic or imperial rulers for their solidarity with the Russian autocrats and their passivity toward them, these campaigns sought to cast doubt about the legitimacy of the rulers. France's rulers, while expressing their sympathy to the Poles (which was genuine in the case of Napoleon the Third, who saw himself as a defender of the principle of nationalities), did not take any action, whether out of fear of war or out of a diplomatic interest in not alienating Russia.

The same solution to the dilemma between supporting East European independence and maintaining good relations with Russia was adopted in this century, from World War I to the Polish crisis in 1981.[3]

Between 1870 and 1945, France's choices were limited by the obvious primacy of the conflict with Germany. The three formal alliances between France and Russia (1893, 1935, and 1945) were all explicitly directed against Germany. Between the time of Bismarck and that of Hitler, the traditional policy of the *alliance de revers* had an obvious necessity to it.

As de Gaulle pointed out when he tried to extend it or to revive it, the policy was based on traditional perceptions both of France's vulnerability and of its potential strength. France was not strong enough to maintain its security alone. It needed to encircle Germany either by a rigid system of alliances (as it tried to do in the interwar period) or by a flexible one. The ultimate danger was an alliance between Germany and Russia as happened with Rapallo and with the Nazi-Soviet pact of 1939. In addition to formal diplomatic and military alliances, France could increase its influence by a superior understanding of basic historical trends, by assuming the mantle of the defender of the aspirations of weaker or emerging nations to independence and freedom (whether in Eastern Europe or, later, in the Third World); France could claim a kind of special authority as a moral umpire of the European and international scene.

It is here that universal principles and ideological considerations fuse with considerations of *Realpolitik*, at least in the case of France.

Much of the debate in the interwar period was couched in balance of power terms (How great was the German danger? How much help could an alliance with the Soviet Union bring?). Even more the debate represented a domestic and ideological cleavage between the right, which feared communism more than nazism, and the left, which favored anti-Fascist unity and for that reason was reluctant to attack the Soviet Union, at least between 1934 and the great shock of the Stalin-Hitler pact of 1939.

It is true that the Franco-Soviet Pact of 1935 was signed by Pierre Laval, who was later to be the pro-German prime minister of the Vichy regime, but was already a right-wing politician. But he did so after long hesitation. The agreement was limited (it lacked military clauses), and it was a direct reaction to Hitler's abandonment of the League of Nations and his decision to rearm. The agreement also had a domestic side, as Laval was happy to embarrass the left and buy Communist toleration, thus setting a pattern that was to be abundantly followed by the governments of the Fifth Republic. After the pact, however, the reluctance of French (and British) conservatives to enter an alliance with the Soviet Union (based partly on ideological reasons, partly on the objections of France's East European allies to Soviet demands to enter their territories) culminated in the Munich Agreement, in which the idea of deflecting Hitler's aggressive intentions from the West to the East was present.

De Gaulle: The Past and the Future

After the war, in the view of some, the traditional game of nations based on national interest, the balance of power, and *alliance de revers* was superseded by the conflict between democracy and totalitarianism, which led to the need for full reconciliation with the newly democratic Federal Republic of Germany and resistance to the only remaining totalitarian threat, the Soviet one. A number of French diplomats, who had participated in the resistance against nazism but also had a firsthand knowledge of Russia, were leading figures in this rethinking, movingly described in a novel by one of them, former ambassador to Moscow and Bonn Henri Froment-Meurice, under the title *A Political Education*. Another, Jean-Marie Soutou, using a formulation by Jacques Bainville, described the primary orientation of the new French policy under the label: "Not to fight the wrong House of Austria," that is, Germany instead of the Soviet Union. Yet another, Jean Laloy, tried, in his book *Entre guerres et paix* (1966) to think through the implications of the obsolescence of traditional power politics. These kinds of views were very important in shaping the policy of the Fourth Republic in the direction represented by Robert Schuman and Jean Monnet. They remain influential within the centrist UDF (Union des Forces Démocratiques).

By contrast, de Gaulle represented a return to the old diplomatic tradition, under new conditions and with new instruments. He practiced the triangular game with a vengeance, in a dazzling succession of combinations always aiming at the same goal: the greatest possible independence for France compared with other nations and for Europe in its relations to the superpowers. During the war, he used the threat of moving his headquarters to Moscow to increase his bargaining power with his Anglo-American allies. During his first tenure in office, in 1944–1946, he eagerly sought a bilateral relationship with a rather contemptuous Stalin and argued that France had common interests with the Soviet Union that it did not share with Britain and the United States. These obviously had to do with Germany. De Gaulle explicitly wanted to prevent an understanding between Germany and its Eastern neighbors and sought, unsuccessfully as it turned out, Soviet support for his German policy, which consisted in dividing Germany into several states and annexing the Saarland.

But his policy was not limited to this narrow German focus. He used the fact that France was not invited to the Yalta Conference to denounce the division of Europe and to launch the mythical charge of a deliberate partition of Europe there for which the superpowers shared the blame equally. This interpretation is so fundamental to the Gaullist stance that at the time of the invasion of Prague, in 1968, de Gaulle claimed it was a necessary consequence of *la politique des blocs* rather than denouncing the Soviet decision as such. This, however, was only the negative side of his "grand design," which also involved overcoming the bipolar order of the superpowers in favor of "another order, another equilibrium" that would be based on an understanding "between Gauls, Slavs, and Germans," with France and Russia being in effect the two pillars of the European order and the Anglo-Saxons (or, at any rate, the United States) being less directly involved.

When he returned to power, in 1958, his former German policy was impossible. But the dream of "Europe from the Atlantic to the Urals" remained alive. New circumstances—the the Sino-Soviet split, the Vietnam war, France's independent nuclear deterrent—made it seem more favorable than before. Only Germany's place had changed both in de Gaulle's tactics and in his vision of a future Europe. Instead of trying to encircle Germany and to prevent its dialogue with the East, he tried to embrace it and to present himself as the promoter and the protector of this very dialogue. Instead of keeping Germany divided into several states, his scheme provided for some form of reassociation between the two German states, under the supervision of "Germany's neighbors." What remained in common, then, was the special Franco-Soviet role, both in the process of "détente, entente et coopération" and in the structure of the new system, where they would act as joint legitimizers and guarantors of the settlement, and, in particular, of the limitations attached to Germany's status.

Beyond Germany, the idea of "Europe from the Atlantic to the Urals" meant that by distancing itself from NATO and working to reduce the American presence in Europe, France would induce Russia, preoccupied as it was with China, to relax its rule and reduce its own presence in Eastern Europe, thereby opening the way to a limited reassertion of national autonomies and of European, particularly French, influence.

The project sometimes seemed to be meant for the long run and to presuppose a degree of West European unity and of Soviet "detotalitarianization" that was far away in de Gaulle's lifetime. Sometimes it appeared to aim at an actual negotiation between Europe, represented by France, and Soviet and East European leaders. In this sense, it clearly had failed by the time of de Gaulle's visit to Poland in 1967 and of Moscow's invasion of Prague in 1968.

As Leonard Brezhnev indicated very clearly to East European leaders, according to Gomulka's interpreter,[4] Moscow saw that de Gaulle's plan was a threat to its hegemony in Eastern Europe: but they also saw, just as clearly, that they could use it for their own purposes, both to split NATO and to legitimize their own rule in the eyes of the Europeans, East and West.[5] They flattered France by systematically encouraging the idea of a special Franco-Soviet relationship between, as they sometimes put it, "the two most powerful countries on the continent," and they tried to inject something of the anti-German tone of 1945 into the relationship. This was not entirely unsuccessful either with de Gaulle or with his successors: each, with the partial exception of Pompidou, has emphasized the priority of the Franco-German friendship, but each has maintained that geography created common security interests between Paris and Moscow, even though the practical results of this thought, besides sowing distrust between Paris and Bonn, are hard to detect.

By contrast, the vision of a Europe overcoming both its artificial division and its dependence upon the superpowers is more alive than ever. While open to debate and to distortion, especially concerning the respective European or non-European character of the two superpowers, this vision continues to inspire the most diverse groups, from East European dissidents to West German writers linked to the SPD, who sometimes complain that it has been more forgotten in France than elsewhere.

It is hard, however, to overestimate de Gaulle's impact on French policy (and even more on French attitudes) toward the Soviet Union. To be sure, none of his successors harbors the illusion of a leading role in East-West relations: whether the dream of French primacy was justified or not in de Gaulle's and Adenauer's time, the Federal Republic and the United States have long since taken détente into their own hands. To be sure, too, French public opinion, at least between the mid-1970s and the mid-1980s, has become more and more sensitive to the totalitarian nature of the Soviet regime and less prone to talk, as de Gaulle did, of "Russia" rather than of "the Soviet Union." The theme of the primacy of national interest over ideology is more popular today in Germany than in France.

Finally, the earth-shaking effect of de Gaulle on the international attitudes of French political forces is beginning to wear out. De Gaulle had forced the traditionally anti-Soviet conservatives to follow him on the path of détente, and had, by the same token, caught the left on the wrong foot, forcing it either to approve his foreign policy or to criticize it on nuclear and disarmament matters or on relations with France's Western allies. In both cases, however, the left had to rally to the Gaullist consensus lest its attachment to France's independence and security be open to doubt. In the 1980s the right has tended to return to its traditional anti-Sovietism while the socialist party, in opposition between 1986 and 1988, has begun to feel a certain nostalgia for the traditional positions of the left on military and nuclear matters. Yet almost nobody, even on the right, would dare question the notion of détente, the necessity of "looking beyond Yalta," or the unacceptability of returning to NATO military integration. Similarly, almost nobody in the Socialist party, as distinct from pro-Communist or leftist groups, dares to question the French nuclear force or to abandon the notions of deterrence and of military balance in favor of disarmament.

Above all, it is the combination of the two—of pursuing détente and challenging Cold War categories and the division of Europe on the one hand and holding firm to nuclear weapons and distrusting superpower détente and regional arms control on the other—that constitutes the peculiarity of the French position. This is entirely due to de Gaulle. The position may be harder and harder to maintain, as first Afghanistan, the SS-20s, and the "new Cold War" made détente look obsolete, and then the "new détente," based essentially on arms control and disarmament makes it more and more difficult to cling to the Gaullist synthesis: if that synthesis was flexible enough to accommodate both the de Gaulle of 1960–64 (the champion of firmness toward the Soviet Union at the time of the Paris summit and the Berlin and Cuba crises) and the de Gaulle of 1964–1968 (the champion of détente and East-West reconciliation), it can accommodate anything except renouncing the goal of national independence.

De Gaulle's Successors

In different ways, de Gaulle's successors tried their hand at adapting the Gaullist framework to changing circumstances. The structure of the French system under the Fifth Republic is such that foreign policy is largely in the hands of the president and of the various bureaucracies, while the parliamentary process, interest groups, and public opinion are far less important.[6] If the president and the bureaucracy agree, other forces have very little chance of affecting the course of foreign policy. Periodically, a new president will try to put his own mark on it and his main adversary will be bureaucratic inertia.

Georges Pompidou's primary interest lay in domestic and Western European affairs. His departure from Gaullist orthodoxy consisted in the admission of Great Britain to the European Economic Community, and in the *relance européenne* of the Hague summit. Yet, precisely because his perspective was more Western-centered, his policy toward the Soviet Union went to considerable lengths in bilateral relations in the name of the triangular game with Germany and the United States. During his tenure, France's role as the pathfinder of détente was exhausted, the dream of "Europe from the Atlantic to the Urals" had vanished, but both had been replaced by the Federal Republic and the United States occupying the center of the East-West stage. Pompidou's policy toward the Soviet Union was essentially reactive. In the first period, in 1970–1972, it was above all a reaction to Germany's *Ostpolitik*, which led it both to try to balance Bonn by a special relationship with London and to avoid a Soviet-German tête-a-tête by keeping up the pretense of a special relationship with Moscow. In the second period, particularly in 1973, it was essentially a reaction to the American-Soviet détente and to the perceived danger of a superpower condominium. This led to a hardening toward the United States, which was accentuated by the "year of Europe" controversy and by the oil crisis, but also toward the Soviet Union. Thus, while at the beginning of his tenure Pompidou had moved toward acceptance of a Conference on Security and Cooperation in Europe (CSCE) (which de Gaulle had opposed) and even toward limited flexibility in the talks on Mutual and Balanced Force Reductions (MBFR), by the end he (through Foreign Minister Michel Jobert) was pouring scorn on the former and opposing the latter more intransigently than ever.

However, this did not detract in the least from the tenacity with which, up till the last moments of his fatal illness, Pompidou was struggling through visits, common declarations, commissions, and protocols on Franco-Soviet relations (even though refusing a formal treaty) in order to maintain the myth of a special, institutionalized, bilateral relationship. In turn, the Soviets, while attacking French policies on many important points, such as West European defense cooperation, respected the person of the French president and continued to go through the motions of pretending that France was their first European interlocutor.

One finds an illustration of these apparent contradictions in the preliminary negotiations for CSCE in Helsinki. The French delegation took the lead in creating and promoting the major innovation of the Helsinki process, the Third Basket, and in organizing cooperation among the members of the European Community. On the other hand, it could less and less escape the dilemma linked to its three partly diverging objectives: encouraging both West European unity and East European independence, while at the same time maintaining a special Franco-Soviet dialogue.

In a different form, similar dilemmas and contradictions were encountered by Valéry Giscard d'Estaing and contributed to his ultimate failure. Giscard d'Estaing was, in a way, the least Gaullist of de Gaulle's successors. He saw the French role more in pleasing and reconciling everybody than in picking fights as de Gaulle and Pompidou (at least in the last Jobertian phase of his presidency) loved to do. He was a true believer in détente less for Gaullist reasons than out of an optimistic view of convergence and interdependence, of the decline of ideology and peace through trade. For the first time, French economic interests and a general view of the impact of economics on politics were at the center of French policy toward the East. The Giscardian belief in the healing powers of modernization might have been most welcome in the Gorbachevian era. As it was, it came too late or too soon. The call for ideological coexistence was abruptly rebuffed by Brezhnev during Giscard's visit to Moscow in 1975 and went more and more against the grain of French public opinion.

Giscard's attitudes themselves were less simple than they seemed. He shared at least some of the classical Gaullist motives for a special Franco-Soviet dialogue. In 1982, in criticizing Mitterrand for letting this dialogue wither away, he wrote: "The direct dialogue of France with the two superpowers, one of them its permanent ally, the other its ideological adversary, is important for three reasons:

- to maintain France's rank at the level of the great powers;
- to participate directly in discussions on peace and the level of armaments;
- finally to avoid the affirmation or confirmation of the supremacy of the Federal Republic of Germany in Europe."[7]

More importantly, a contrast can be found between Giscard's attitudes in direct dealings with the Soviet Union particularly in Europe, and in opposition to Soviet influence in the Third World, particularly in Africa. On the one hand, he went to extraordinary lengths to avoid offending the Soviet Union or compromising détente: well-known examples are his cold attitude to Soviet dissidents; refusing to receive Andre Amalrik and allowing his prime minister, Jacques Chirac, to chide Leonid Plioutsch for abusing French hospitality by attacking the Soviet regime; his coolness to the Afghan resistance and to the Polish Solidarity movement (his meeting with Brezhnev in Warsaw at the height of the Afghan crisis and his triumphant report that, thanks to his influence, the Soviets had started withdrawing); his accusing the Carter administration of breaking détente; and his refusal to use his influence in favor of boycotting the Moscow Olympics. On the other hand, in the Congo, he took the lead, with American help, in opposing a real or imagined danger of Communist subversion and, in the fights within the Carter administration, he clearly favored the hard line of Zbigniew Brzezinski against that of Cyrus Vance.

Michel Tatu attributes this contrast to domestic reasons. He sees a hardening of Giscard's line on East-West relations in the middle period of his presidency and a markedly pro-Soviet turn during the last year, inspired by the hope of tacit Soviet support in the 1981 presidential election. There is no doubt that this hope existed, and was reasonable given the strong evidence that it had indeed been forthcoming for his election in 1974 as well as for Pompidou's in 1969 and for de Gaulle's reelection in 1965. But another reason may be deeper and more important. It is the contrast between words and deeds. In deeds, particularly in the military field, Giscard had been as willing to take steps opposed by the Soviet Union as any of his predecessors or successors. He increased the defense budget and took rather daring steps to bring French defense closer to NATO and to enhance Franco-German defense cooperation. He increased de facto cooperation with NATO, particularly in naval matters. But he always insisted on compensating these actions with a declaratory policy reaffirming détente and attempting to placate the Soviet Union. In a famous press conference of May 1975, to which Raymond Aron attached the infamous label of "voluntary Finlandization," he said that the theme of West European defense, which would be, one day, a natural conse-quence of Europe's political union, should not be prematurely discussed in public lest it attract understandable Soviet objections because of the German problem. It had to be prepared within a political environment that made it acceptable to the East as well as to the West.

This statement, and Giscard's whole attitude, can be seen as a legitimate and sophisticated application of a combination of defense and détente. But it was too clever by half. Giscard's soothing discourse, besides showing a certain lack of moral and psychological sensitivity, did more to irritate his followers and allies than to reassure his adversaries. It had fallen out of line both with the domestic mood and with the harsher choices imposed, after 1979, by an international environment dominated by the SS-20 missiles, the Soviet invasion of Afghanistan, and the Polish crisis.

Mitterrand: From Change to Continuity?

It has often been remarked that each American administration starts by claiming to do the exact opposite of its predecessor, only to end up returning to the old policy. Something like that happened with the arrival in power of Mitterrand, at least in the area of East-West relations. (In nuclear matters, continuity was stressed from the beginning.) In his first phase, from 1981 to 1983, he abruptly broke the comfortable institutionalization of the Franco-Soviet special relationship. He became the most prominent spokesman in Europe of the hard line toward the Soviet Union. After 1983, and more particularly in 1985 and 1986, he started mending his fences with Moscow, advocating new positive developments in East-West relations, and a constructive French role in bringing them about. After March 1986, cohabitation with the Chirac government ushered a new period, but one in which the differences that existed between President Mitterrand and Prime Minister Chirac took on a more "Gaullist" line, in the sense of de Gaulle's détente policy as well as of the primacy of the national deterrent over West European cooperation, than did the Gaullists and centrists who were running the government. During 1987 and 1988, and more particularly during the months preceding the spring 1988 presidential elections, a real shift in Mitterrand's attitudes on the main East-West issues seems to have taken place. Before examining the reasons for these shifts and considering the extent to which they offer a clue to future trends and cleavages, it is worth recapitulating briefly what actually happened.

In a sense, the change occurred before the socialists came to power. In the 1970s, the socialists had been trying to dispel the Soviet distrust toward them by taking a more pro-détente line than Pompidou and Giscard, whether on the issue of a Franco-Soviet treaty or on arms control. During visits to Moscow and Budapest in 1975, they were lavish with praise of the positive role of the Soviet Union in world affairs. However, at the end of the decade, Mitterrand was one of the first politicians to denounce the threat posed by the SS-20s. He even went beyond NATO's two-track decision by suggesting reestablishing the balance *before* negotiating in order to dismantle both the Pershings and the SS-20s. During the electoral campaign he castigated Giscard d'Estaing for playing "the messenger boy," as the first Western statesman to meet with Brezhnev on Afghanistan in the summer of 1980.

Once in power, Mitterrand acted very quickly in the directions indicated by his criticisms. He stopped the mechanism of yearly Franco-Soviet meetings, on the grounds that normal Franco-Soviet relations were impossible as long as the Soviet behavior in Afghanistan and Poland did not change; and he took a position in favor of NATO's double decision on the missile deployments, whereas Giscard d'Estaing, who had helped engineer the decision, had avoided supporting it in public for fear of making it easier for the Soviet Union to involve the French nuclear force in arms control negotiations.

This phase culminated in early 1983, with Mitterrand's speech at the Bundestag in January in favor of the deployment of the missiles and more generally in favor of maintaining the military balance and nuclear deterrence. This is also the period when he was campaigning against pacifism with the slogan: "The missiles are in the East and the pacifists are in the West." In 1983 the spectacular expulsion of forty-seven Soviet diplomats or pseudo-diplomats for industrial spying (resulting from a discovery by French intelligence that was communicated to the United States) symbolized the new French toughness.

Yet already in this first period, important nuances and qualifications, if not outright contradictions, were apparent. French policy under the socialists has displayed a contrast between a strong anti-Soviet and pro-Atlanticist position where the direct Soviet military threat in Europe has been concerned, and strong criticism of American policy in the Third World as well as sympathy for the more romantic revolutionary regimes, particularly the Cuban and the Nicaraguan ones.

In Europe and in relations with the Soviet Union, what changed above all under Mitterrand was the rhetoric of French policy, its emphasis on human rights, the importance given to Soviet and East European dissidents, and the readiness to condemn Soviet actions. But from the beginning it was reluctant to back up the strong rhetoric with any tangible deeds. In particular, Mitterrand has always been as opposed as Giscard d'Estaing to the use of the economic weapon. He signed the controversial gas pipeline deal with the Soviet Union within weeks of General Jaruzelski's coup, refused to follow the United States in imposing sanctions against Poland (although France did take a harder line on the Polish debt than the Federal Republic), and got into a serious conflict with the United States over the issue of technology embargoes aimed at the Soviet Union. Mitterrand revived the theme of Yalta and reaffirmed the goal of overcoming the division of Europe but warned, at the same time, that one should not underestimate "the slowness of history." To many, then, he appeared to have more a slogan than a policy and to believe in the magic power of words where others were using carrots or sticks. It is debatable whether the contrast between words and deeds was putting France in an embarrassing and slightly ridiculous situation or whether, on the contrary, by proclaiming the truth about the situation in Europe or in the Third World even though it could take no practical steps about it, France was fulfilling an important task and following the best of its traditions.

At any rate, as in the case of the Carter administration, such a stand could not be sustained indefinitely. In 1983, the signs multiplied that the cooling off of relations was just, to use the expression of one of Mitterrand's advisers, a temporary *cure de desintoxication* and, anyway, had concerned only the institutionalization and regularity of meetings, not the normal course of relations, which had never been broken. After the downing of the Korean airliner, a visit by Mr. Gromyko to Paris was postponed by only a few days and France was the first country to receive a high-level Soviet official, just as, in 1980, Giscard d'Estaing had been the first Western statesman to meet Brezhnev after the invasion of Kabul, and Mitterrand was to be the first head of state to receive Jaruzelski in 1985.

In 1984, 1985, and 1986, there were three meetings between Mitterrand and Gorbachev, thereby reestablishing the old pattern. In 1984, Mitterrand went to Moscow but made it a point to raise publicly, in his Kremlin toast, the then taboo issue of Sakharov. In 1985, Gorbachev stopped in Paris on the way to his Geneva summit with Reagan, thereby nodding in the direction of the old special relationship with Paris. But the meeting was much less euphoric than Gorbachev's earlier trip to London, and Mitterrand made no concession on including the French nuclear force in the arms control process, an issue that appears more and more central to Franco-Soviet relations.

In 1986, Mitterrand visited Moscow again, after having seen President Reagan in Washington, thereby suggesting (although formally denying it) the role of intermediary (if not of "messenger boy") between the two superpowers. But the most striking feature of the visit was his warm praise of Gorbachev's modern vision and reformist intentions.

This contrasted in tone if not in substance with the formulations of the new Chirac government, particularly of its foreign minister, former ambassador to Moscow Jean-Bernard Raimond, who coined the slogan of the "double vigilance:" to be alert to possible changes for the better in Soviet policy but equally to traps and to the danger of making unilateral concessions.

In practice no real differences on East-West relations appeared between the government and the president (unlike on North-South relations), except a certain upgrading of relations with the Afghan resistance, until the spring of 1987. Then, however, on the "double-zero option" that Reagan and Gorbachev negotiated, a clear split emerged between Mitterrand (who firmly supported the first one, on long-range intermediary nuclear forces and implicitly assented to the second one on short-range intermediary nuclear forces) and part of the government, in particular Defense Minister Giraud (who called the whole proposal a trap whose acceptance would mean a new Munich). Other centrists outside the government, in particular Raymond Barre, took a position similar to Giraud's.

Prime Minister Chirac and Foreign Minister Raimond tried to find a middle position, accepting the first-zero option but trying to replace the second by an European proposal based on an "intermediary solution." This collapsed in mid-May 1987 because of international and domestic pressures on Margaret Thatcher and Helmut Kohl; but a contributing factor to Kohl's following his Foreign Minister Hans-Dietrich Genscher rather than his conservative friends had been Mitterrand's discreet but unequivocal stand in favor of the agreement proposed by Gorbachev. Chirac had to rally to this position, both for constitutional reasons and because he could not allow Mitterrand a monopoly on the dialogue with the East. His own trip to Moscow, also in May 1987, almost did not take place through Soviet ill will, but finally was a relative success since, like Thatcher a few weeks before, and like Mitterrand in 1984, he showed he could maintain a cordial tone (and obtain some economic results) while remaining firm both on arms control and on human rights (he mentioned Afghanistan and met a group of refuseniks).

In the second half of 1987 and the spring of 1988, divergences came more and more into the open, largely under the initiative of Mitterrand. They concerned attitudes toward Gorbachev. While Foreign Minister Raimond was insisting on the need for "double vigilance" (positive and negative), Mitterrand was more and more stressing the positive. In an interview with the Soviet daily *Izvestia* on December 2, 1987, Mitterrand quoted approvingly a famous and controversial formula by the French statesman Georges Clemenceau about the French Revolution ("The Revolution is one bloc") and applied it to the Soviet one. He later qualified this judgment that seemed to justify Lenin's and Stalin's terrorist excesses.[9] On the other hand, he never withdrew his positive reaction to Gorbachev's arms control initiatives; the Soviet leader "was right a hundred times" to propose the zero option on intermediate nuclear forces, he said in a campaign interview, and President Reagan was right to accept it. Against the quasi-unanimity of the French political class, which was shocked by the Reyjkavik summit and indignantly denounced the collusion between the two superpowers, he hailed the prospects of superpower détente and disarmament as long as they were balanced. As for the dangers of decoupling between the United States and Europe, he claimed they were to be found not in the disappearance of short- or medium-range weapons from the continent but in the strategy of flexible response, which meant the abandonment of deterrence in favor of limited war.

He seemed, then, to depart in two basic ways from the Gaullist consensus. On the one hand, security was to be found in disarmament rather than in nuclear deterrence. The dilemma he wanted to confront voters with was: Was the arms race leading to war or disarmament leading to peace?—with no possible middle ground. On the other hand, while he was stressing the building of Europe as his grand design for the future of France, this grand design was not directed to the self-assertion of European independence against the danger of superpower condominium. By downgrading both the importance of theater nuclear weapons and the prospects for European nuclear collaboration and modernization, the French national deterrent and the European community were both made apparently compatible with Gorbachev's "Common European House."

How did this change come to pass? How lasting is it likely to be? What impact is it likely to have on the prospects for a joint Western or European policy toward the East? For a tentative answer to these questions, we must return to the various factors we distinguished at the beginning. Almost as much as in the case of de Gaulle, the last, personal factor is essential: it is through the perception, the objectives, and the strategy of one man, in this case François Mitterrand, that international and domestic realities are translated into policy.

In May 1981, it is likely that his decision to change French policy toward the Soviet Union was motivated by four sets of considerations that happened to converge. Two were international: Mitterrand's view of the state of the East-West balance and of the trend in Germany's evolution. Two were domestic: his assessment of the mechanics of party alliances and of the trend in French public opinion. The East-West balance—after America's defeat in Vietnam, the hesitations of the Carter administration, Moscow's progress in the Third World, and, above all, its invasion of Afghanistan and growing military presence in Europe—was seen as tilting dangerously toward Moscow, and thus as necessitating a balancing effort from the Europeans. In particular, Mitterrand saw the SS-20s as posing a novel and unacceptable threat to West European security.

Like most Frenchmen, Mitterrand was impressed by the progress of antinuclear and anti-American feelings in Germany. He feared that, combined with the declining credibility of America's engagement, it would lead to a Germany sliding into neutralism, which would create dangers of Soviet domination and French isolation. Hence he thought it was necessary to do what he could to anchor the Federal Republic firmly in the West, both by creating more of a feeling of common West European commitment and by encouraging Atlantic unity rather than centrifugal American and German trends.

Domestically, having made the alliance with the Communist party and its participation in government into a crucial element of his strategy for bringing the left into power and then transforming it by strengthening the Socialist party at the expense of the Communists, he had to reassure the worried, uncommitted voters and, even more, France's Western allies (particularly the United States and the Federal Republic, whose trust was indispensable for financial as well as for security reasons) that he was not their prisoner. Conversely, his support for revolution in the Third World was based both on genuine belief and on the domestic need to reassure the socialist true believers that he had not entirely sold out to the Americans and that he was fighting the American economic and cultural danger as well as the Soviet military one.

Finally, French public opinion, after having become more favorable to the Soviet Union during the years of détente and de-Stalinization, had become more and more hostile since the decline of détente in the mid-1970s. We have already mentioned the evolution of left-wing intellectuals, which culminated with the rise of the "new philosophers."[10]

Hence a temporary anti-Soviet alliance came into being between some rather strange bedfellows: Mitterrand, who was moved essentially by his own calculations of domestic and international balance, and a French public opinion that, particularly in the non-Communist left, was following essentially moral and ideological motivations.

This alliance was shattered as early as January 1982 when, after a month of national unanimity in support of *Solidarity*, the French government disappointed the "antitotalitarian left" by its failure to follow a policy of sanctions. But the real separation came with the second phase of Mitterrand's policy, after 1983–1984.

In that period all the elements of the 1981 consensus had changed except French public opinion. In the French view, the Soviet danger was as great as ever. For Mitterrand, however, a number of developments, international and national, called for "rebalancing" in the direction opposite to the 1981 one. The first was the Reagan effect and, in particular, SDI. Now it was the United States that, politically and militarily, was on the offensive, and seemed to be, technologically, one age ahead of the rest of the world. The Soviet Union appeared to be paralyzed both by the age of its leaders and by the inefficiency of the system.[11] More specifically, while with the SS-20s the Soviets were endangering French and European security, the United States, with SDI, was also posing threats of obsolescence to the French nuclear deterrent and of decoupling from Europe, thereby creating a common interest between France and the Soviet Union. Finally, once the deployment of the Pershing IIs and cruise missiles had begun, the danger of imbalance in Europe was coming from the Americans since the Pershings were creating a new threat, one as unacceptable to the Soviet Union as the SS-20s were to the West. Mitterrand seems to be a true believer in a quantitative equilibrium at every level. In this sense, there is no contradiction between his earlier campaign against the SS-20s and for the deployments and his favorable attitude to the zero option.

On Germany, again, Kohl's victory in the national elections and the beginning of the deployments seemed to demonstrate that the danger of German pacifism and neutralism had ended. Conversely, SDI and a number of cases in which the Federal Republic in its policies of arms cooperation seemed to give too great a priority to its American connection over its French one, seemed to raise again the older French worry of an excessively rather than an insufficiently pro-American Federal Republic.

Another international reason for reopening the dialogue with the Soviet Union was economic, as France's deficit increased. Domestically, the Communist exit from the government further liberated Mitterrand from the need for anti-Soviet credentials. In general, his perception seems to have been that both the French stance on the deployments and the failure of the Soviet and pacifist campaign against them were a turning point after which there was no longer any need to take an anti-Soviet stance. He seems to have underestimated both the permanence of the double problem raised by the INF issue (that of the role of the U.S. and of nuclear weapons in Europe and particularly in Germany) and the resilience of the antitotalitarian mood in French society. His reception of Jaruzelski in December 1985 (done in a clumsy and embarrassed way) was denounced by a great majority of public opinion and by the whole political élite, from his own Prime Minister Laurent Fabius to Raymond Barre, who saw a golden opportunity to rejoin the mainstream without bringing with him any disadvantages internationally.

In the new phase, which is unfolding at the time of this writing, conditions may have changed more fundamentally. They seem to give François Mitterrand both a better reason for a shift in policies and a better chance of carrying French public opinion with him. But they also pose the danger of breaking the French consensus and of compromising France's view of its European role.

The Gorbachev Challenge

The new factors that intervened in 1985–1987 are, in the East-West area, the decline of Reagan and the rise of Gorbachev and, in the domestic area, cohabitation and the 1988 presidential elections. But the effects of the first two factors on the German and European public opinion, including, for the first time, the French one, may be the most important of all both in Mitterrand's calculations and for future trends and options.

Paradoxically, Gorbachev's spectacular political Blitzkrieg and Reagan's decline seem to lead Mitterrand to the opposite analysis than the one in 1983–1984 but to the same conclusion, that is, the favoring of détente and of a revival of Franco-Soviet relations (as distinct from the first period in 1981–1983). Instead of a dangerously assertive and adventuristic America and a Soviet Union so paralyzed as to no longer represent an immediate danger, the world confronted a paralyzed America and a Soviet leader so dynamic and attractive as to be virtually irresistible. France, in this view, would only isolate itself by playing the spoiler. Mitterrand seems to believe that superpower détente and arms control will dominate the coming period and that

France has to learn to play the new game. This is reinforced by two sets of considerations, one concerning the evolution of Germany and the other the fate of the French nuclear deterrent.

After having first feared German neutralism and then opposed German Atlanticism, Mitterrand seems to believe that under the new conditions the Genscher line is the only possible one for the Federal Republic. Whatever the grumblings of his own party, Chancellor Kohl cannot resist the joint pressures of the superpowers and of German public opinion against nuclear weapons and for détente. Hence rearguard actions against the "double-zero option" or stern warnings on the model of Mitterrand's Bundestag speech are unrealistic, and they are unnecessary as long as a quantitative balance is maintained. The aim is not to leave Germany alone in its dialogue with the superpowers, particularly with the East.

What counts above all, on the other hand, is to preserve the French nuclear force. For this, a certain goodwill toward Gorbachev in order to buy his tolerance is needed, and this may involve the sacrifice of French tactical nuclear weapons in order to save the strategic ones. At any rate, while progress on European defense, and particularly on Franco-German military cooperation, is highly desirable, it is best limited to conventional forces. France should stay clear both of a nuclear guarantee to Germany and of getting too committed in pleading for the preservation of an American nuclear presence on the continent. In effect, in spite of genuine efforts in the European direction, this does amount to a withdrawal into the French nuclear sanctuary combined with (and protected by) détente.

This is rather reminiscent in some ways of the Gaullist period, in others of Giscard's positions. Conversely, if not Giscard himself at least most of his centrist friends, with Raymond Barre as well as most of the Gaullists, believe that the reaction to the new situation should be to denounce the denuclearization of Europe and to fight for a European nuclear deterrent.

This is less paradoxical than it seems, provided one does not forget the domestic dimension. The Socialist party cannot completely forgo the traditional left-wing themes of disarmament and social priorities versus the arms race—especially at a time of budgetary constraints. Short of appearing unpatriotic, the defense of these themes has to rely on a positive appraisal of the international situation and on a downgrading of the Soviet military threat. Conversely, the conservatives have to guard against their followers listening to the accusation of the extreme right that they are "soft on communism." They have to raise the specter of the left leading to Finlandization: the curious turning of the tables between Barre and Mitterrand on INF and relations with Moscow has something to do with the fact that they play to different audiences.

What this would seem to mean, then, is that a certain polarization along right versus left lines is in the making on defense and East-West issues. But the new and more important factor, which transcends party lines, is to be found in the public opinion polls, which seem to indicate that the famous and unique French consensus is being seriously weakened.

Beyond a basic belief in independence and in the necessity of military balance, this consensus had three pillars: the Gaullist belief in nuclear deterrence, the antitotalitarian distrust of the Soviet Union, and the more recent pro-capitalist fashion favorable to the United States and to the Reagan administration.[12] Now all three of these elements are weakened. The belief in nuclear energy has been shattered by Chernobyl. The distrust toward the Soviet Union is being weakened by Gorbachev. The belief in the United States and in particular in the Reagan administration, has been damaged by Reyjkavik and Irangate.

In none of the three cases does one witness a radical change. America is still much more popular than the Soviet Union, there still is no real antinuclear movement in France, and the public is still, by a large majority, favorable to keeping the nuclear deterrent and to moving forward a European nuclear defense. But on all these issues (except the European one), the majority is smaller and the discordant voices louder.

The most important change is the reaction to Gorbachev and its impact on the image of the Soviet Union. France remains the least pro-Gorbachevian country in Europe. Forty-three percent of the French believe that his will to change the system is genuine (against 66 percent as a European average), and 38 percent believe that the United States is more peace-loving than the Soviet Union (against 22 percent in Germany). Fifty-three percent against 28 percent favor the zero option, whereas the German figure is 85 percent. The image of the Soviet Union remains a negative one for 59 percent against 18 percent of the public, and is particularly so among the young.

Yet the fact remains that, for the first time since Khrushchev, a Soviet leader has a positive image and, more importantly, the French judgment of the Soviet Union, while still negative, is becoming less so. As for the zero option, a strong minority has become a slight majority in its favor.[13]

These results would seem to show that, as in 1981 but in the opposite direction, Mitterrand has sensed (or anticipated in 1985) the direction of public opinion that was crystallized by Gorbachev and that his conservative opponents were swimming against the tide. Where will this tide carry France's position and policies, particularly regarding the Soviet Union, the Western Alliance, and the orientation of Europe?

It could conceivably go far enough to cancel much that this chapter has described. The convergence of the Gorbachev and Mitterrand factors may be powerful enough to wipe out, for all practical purposes, not only what has been called the "Solzhenitsyn factor," the anti-Soviet consensus of the last ten to fifteen years, but also the de Gaulle factor, the set of institutions and attitudes identified with the Fifth Republic itself.

If Gorbachev stays in power, if his course is not blocked or abruptly changed by events, Soviet relations with the rest of the world will enter a new phase based on détente and arms control. Moscow will try to seduce rather than to frighten. This phase will be more far-reaching and resilient than earlier ones. Even if, as seems more likely than not, Gorbachev's reforms do not succeed in shaking the Soviet economy into efficiency but do succeed only too well in shaking Soviet or East European society into turmoil, thereby leading either to revolution or to regression and repression, it seems likely that something of the current changes in the international image and foreign policies of the Soviet Union will remain. Moscow is not likely to fascinate Europeans again by its ideological appeal or to terrorize them again by its nuclear threat. Even if it starts looking more attractive or more powerful or both, its appeal and its power are likely to be more ambiguous than during the old Cold War. On the other hand, a coalition between Genscher's Free Democrats and the SPD is more likely than not to reach power in Bonn sometime during the 1990s, and Mrs. Thatcher will one day be replaced by the Labor party in Britain.

Whether or not these developments coincide, and particularly if they are combined with a decrease in American troops and nuclear weapons on the continent, the chances are more than negligible of progress toward Gorbachev's "Common European House," that is toward a Europe whose security is based more on cooperation than on a military balance, where the nuclear factor and the American influence become less important while Western Europe fails to build its own deterrent.

Until now France has played the spoiler or the Cassandra, warning against the dangers of this trend and vowing to oppose it, preferably together with others but alone if necessary. Francois Mitterrand seems less and less inclined to stick to this attitude. What his triumphant reelection to a seven-year term as president indicates is that he may be able to go beyond a temporary or tactical change of emphasis toward a historic change in France's position and role.

The reason is that just as France's proud stubbornness under the Fifth Republic (with the passing and partial exception of the Giscard d'Estaing period) was matched by Soviet rigidity, so, conversely, the flexibility introduced by Gorbachev in Soviet foreign policy and the restructuring he promotes in Soviet society may encounter Mitterrand's new flexibility in foreign affairs and the restructuring of French political life both demonstrated and encouraged by his triumph.

In a way, the magnitude of his victory confirms and accentuates the main feature of the Fifth Republic—the power of the president. As he fulfills his dream of matching de Gaulle's length of tenure and personal authority, Mitterrand is free, like de Gaulle, to change France's foreign policy course and to try to shape a new domestic consensus. The more his situation resembles de Gaulle's the more he is free, unlike all his predecessors, including himself, to ignore de Gaulle's ghost and the sacred principles and attitudes bestowed on France by him. This is all the more so since the objective constraints are weaker for Mitterrand, at least domestically and in the short run, than they were for de Gaulle.

And here is the second feature of the paradox. While in the short run the power of the president is more like de Gaulle's structurally, in the longer run the presidential elections of 1988 signify the end of the Fifth Republic and, in a way, a return to the Fourth, with the possible influence on foreign policy of the combination of domestic and international political forces.

Ever since World War II, France's special posture in international affairs rested in great part upon the existence of two major organized popular forces: the Communists and the Gaullists. The center, the non-Gaullist far right like the Poujade movement, the non-Communist left with Mendes-France, the liberal-conservatives with Giscard d'Estaing, broad social movements like that of May 1968, all came and went. The two pillars of the system, the Communist and the Gaullist, always reemerged either under the Fourth Republic, in joint opposition (as with the defeat of the European Defense Community project in 1954), or under the Fifth, with one of them in power and the other in opposition but exercising a tacit veto over the policies of the first. This is one key to the contrasting attitudes of the Gaullist governments and of the first Mitterrand presidency toward the Soviet Union.

Now, both communism and Gaullism, which have been declining since 1968, have almost completed their collapse: for the Communists, the collapse started accelerating with the presidential elections of 1981, and those of 1988 seemed to deliver the last blow, although the parliamentary elections that followed in June showed that the news of the French Communist party's death were vastly exaggerated. For the Gaullists, Giscard d'Estaing's presidency was the first warning, but Chirac's defeat, the fragmentation of the center-right, the emergence of the Le Pen extremist movement signify a probably irreversible blow to the Gaullist attempt at uniting and controlling the right. The prospects are for a long dominance of the left, around the Socialist party, with the right being kept from power by its own division and by the dilemmas of its relations with Le Pen. This, of course, would be the mirror image of the long domination of the right, with the left kept from power before Mitterrand by its divisions and by the dilemmas of its relations with the Communist party. But this means that, with the two forces that stood for a particular position in international affairs being excluded, France becomes much more like its neighbors, except for the greater force of populist protest and of the extreme right, and much more open to outside influences, particularly from the left.

This may create, for the first time, the conditions for a Western consensus on policies toward the East or, on the contrary, for a polarization within the Alliance along left versus right or détente versus defense lines. The question is whether there is still room for a specific French role that would preserve and adapt some of de Gaulle's ideas while abandoning his attempts to go it alone. France would articulate a new consensus with an eye toward overcoming the twin dangers of European passivity and polarization.

The trend in Europe is toward détente on the basis of opposition to nuclear weapons and ideological convergence. Against this, a minority, usually on the right, is sticking to a negative position, denouncing Gorbachev as a fraud and denying any change in the Soviet regime and any decrease in the Soviet threat.

What seems endangered in the post-Reykjavik world is a position that would maintain the value of nuclear deterrence and the importance of the opposition between freedom and communism, yet would recognize both the need for other types of defense and the importance of working to overcome both Europe's dependence upon the superpowers and its division. This, however, is the valid part of the Gaullist message. France is still the country most faithful to a vision of international order that includes "old" elements like balance and deterrence, freedom and human rights, and "new" ones like the need to overcome the cleavages between East and West and between North and South.

While the decline of French exceptionalism is inevitable and in many ways desirable, it is to be hoped that abandoning the illusion of a special leading role as an interlocutor of the Soviet Union will not mean leaving the role of articulating a European vision to Mr. Gorbachev.

Notes

1. See J. Becker, "Le modèle soviétique et l'opinion française" and R. Girault, "La France et les autres: les enjeux de la modernisation," in *La France en voie de modernisation : 1944–1952*, a conference held at the Foundation Nationale des Sciences Politiques, mimeo., 1981.
2. J. Michelet, "Pologne et Russie," *Oeuvres Completes*, Vol. XVI, Paris: Flammarion.
3. See J.N. Jeannenney, "1831–1863–1861, La Pologne ecrasée et la France impuissante," *Le Monde*, July 18, 1987.
4. E. Weit, *L'ombre de Gomulka*, Paris: Laffont, 1971.
5. See Michel Jobert interview in A. Wilkens, *La Politique francaise à l'egard de l'Union soviétique pendant la présidence de Georges Pompidou (1969–1974)*. Memoire pour le DEA en Science Politique, Paris, mimeo., Sept. 1984.
6. See my "The View from Paris," in Lincoln Gordon, ed., *Eroding Empire*, Washington: Brookings, 1987, pp. 209–213.
7. V. Giscard d'Estaing, "Ou va la France? Le recul," *Le Figaro*, June 21, 1982.
8. See M. Tatu, "Valéry Giscard d'Estaing et la détente," chapter 8, pp. 196–217 in *La politique extérieure de Valéry Giscard d'Estaing*, edited by S. Cohen and M.C. Smouts, Paris: Presses de la Foundation Nationale des Sciences Politiques, 1985, and my comments in the same book, chapter 10, "Les Mots et les choses," pp. 232–241.
9. See *Commentaire*, XI, 41, Spring 1988, pp. 346–347.
10. See my studies "Western European Perceptions of the Soviet Union," *Daedalus*, Winter 1979, and "Soviet Totalitarianism: The Transatlantic Vagaries of a Concept," *The Washington Quarterly*, Fall 1985.
11. This is the vision in Régis Debray's book, *Les Empires contre l'Europe*, Paris: Gallimard, 1985. While Debray's ideas are not necessarily identical with Mitterrand's, the publication of his book must have been authorized by the French president, for whom he was working at the time.
12. See Denis Lacorne, Jacques Rupnik, and Marie-France Toinet, eds., *De l'anti-américanisme à l'américanophilie*, Paris: Hachette, 1986.
13. See Sofres, "Les Français, le disarmament et l'Union soviétique," a poll conducted by A. Duhamel, Paris, mimeo., July 1987.

Britain and the Soviet Union

Edwina Moreton

"The relationship between Britain and the Soviet Union has never been easy and rarely stable. It has run in the course of nearly seventy years the full range from undeclared war to formal alliance, from the reality of nuclear confrontation to the search for a realistic détente. The problem of establishing a sound relationship between states pursuing conflicting ideologies is as difficult for today's policy-makers as it was for their predecessors in the early years after the October revolution."[1]

Such was the recent judgment of the first British parliamentary report on Anglo-Soviet relations. That the House of Commons foreign affairs committee should have chosen to make the Soviet Union the subject of only its second major investigation was testimony to the reawakening of interest in the Soviet Union and its policies in the ill-tempered years of East-West relations in the early 1980s. The committee produced its report after Mikhail Gorbachev had assumed power in the Kremlin, but before he had had much chance to lay out his program of domestic and foreign policy. Yet, it is doubtful that the committee would have found much to alter if the report had been issued later. The somber note struck by the committee is testimony to the hostility that has characterized British-Soviet relations in the past and the caution that still attaches to them.

Until East-West relations went sour in the late 1970s and early 1980s, even a well-informed visitor to Britain might have concluded that Britain barely had a relationship with the Soviet Union. Increasingly outdone in trade by its continental European partners, increasingly preoccupied with its loss of empire, its special relationship with America, and its gradual readjustment to the political geography of the Europe of the EEC, Britain clearly had other issues and other countries uppermost in its mind. Yet, appearance can be deceptive. Britain's attitude toward the Soviet Union may not have dominated the headlines of the 1960s and 1970s, but successive British governments' assumptions about the Soviet Union have formed the foundation-stone of Britain's foreign policy since World War II.

Simply put, for the past forty years the Soviet Union has been seen and addressed as the chief external threat to British security. This was the rationale for the maintenance of NATO and for Britain's role within it. That Britain chose to deal with this perceived threat to its security through the multilateral framework of the Western Alliance should not obscure the importance of that threat in coloring British attitudes toward the Soviet Union, or in guiding British foreign policy. Policy toward the Soviet Union may have been largely multilateral in thrust, but its content seemed to serve national interests well enough. The broad consensus on security issues and attitudes to the Soviet Union in the British parliament between successive governments and successive oppositions rendered British policy toward the Soviet Union less newsworthy but no less crucial. The unremarkable rule of thumb was: negotiate where useful results can be achieved, contain where necessary. For most of the years of NATO's existence, this approach has coincided happily with the broad consensus within the Alliance.

As was the case elsewhere in Europe, the British parliament's apparently dormant interest in Soviet foreign policy was jolted into life by the Soviet invasion of Afghanistan in December 1979 and by the Polish crisis of 1980–1981. It was sustained by the shift of gears in the British government's own *Ostpolitik* following these two crises in East-West relations. As Sir Geoffrey Howe, the British foreign secretary, confirmed in a speech at the Royal Institute of International Affairs in London on May 7, 1987, the Thatcher government at the start of its second term in 1983 had made it a priority of its foreign policy to work for an improvement in East-West relations.[2] But why would the most openly anti-Communist and at times most stridently anti-Soviet British prime minister since the 1950s make relations with the Soviet Union a high priority?

The policy has certainly had some dramatic results. The pictures of the "Iron Lady" shaking hands in the Kremlin with Mikhail Gorbachev in the spring of 1987 confirmed that. It evidently did Mrs. Thatcher no harm, in the approach of a general election at home, to be seen hobnobbing with the new leader in the Kremlin. She clearly enjoys her reputation as Europe's longest-serving and most experienced prime minister. Yet there is much more to this reactivation of Anglo-Soviet relations than merely a prime minister's political vanity.

There is a third reason that Anglo-Soviet relations have returned to the front pages of the newspapers. In the spring of 1987, as the "Iron Lady" metamorphosed before the Moscow television cameras into the

"Lady with Blue Eyes," the images of Anglo-Soviet diplomatic harmony temporarily turned attention away from an underlying shift in British politics: the breakdown of the traditional bipartisan approach of the British House of Commons to security and defense issues. Since the Soviet Union has traditionally been seen as the greatest postwar threat to Britain's security, a change in attitudes to defense, combined with an improving relationship with the Soviet Union, at least raises the question of whether traditional British security policy and attitudes to the Soviet Union will themselves undergo significant change.

The Historical Elements of British Policy

Of course, Anglo-Soviet rivalries and differences go back a long way. As two empires with conflicting interests, relations were no better than cautious even before the Crimean War of 1854–1856 brought the two imperial powers into direct conflict. Indeed the British image of Russia as the "bogeyman" of Europe is very much a nineteenth-century one. After the Crimean War, relations had all the frostiness of the modern Cold War. This old grating of empires has little practical relevance to Anglo-Soviet relations in the modern era, especially since Britain's pullback from its global role East of Suez in the late 1960s. Yet every so often there is a flash of *Schadenfreude* to British attitudes, for example following the Soviet blunder into Afghanistan in 1979—once a cockpit for imperial rivalries—and the subsequent damage that costly war did to Soviet foreign policy.

In the early part of the twentieth century, a different Russian specter haunted British foreign policy interests, that of Soviet communism. Before the end of World War II, Britain had gone from intervention against the newly formed Bolshevik state in order to prevent Russia's withdrawal from World War I against Germany, to the World War II alliance with the Soviet Union against Germany after the German invasion of Russia in 1941. Throughout this period relations had been marked on the British side by a mix of ideological distaste and pragmatic necessity. The Russian revolution was, from the British point of view, at best ill-timed, at worst a direct challenge to the world order that had served Britain so well and left it in charge of a world-spanning empire. After the revolution, Britain's attitude to the Soviet Union was very much a function of its need to keep Germany in check and its own mercantile interests secure. Thus, it is hardly surprising that, despite all that had passed before, Churchill's first reaction to the news of the German attack on Russia in 1941 was to offer Stalin all possible assistance against the country that once again had become common enemy number one. Or, as Churchill himself put it more memorably in explaining his change of heart: "I have only one purpose, the destruction of Hitler, and my life is much simplified thereby. If Hitler invaded hell I would make at least a favorable reference to the Devil in the House of Commons."

Obviously, Britain's security was to be the paramount consideration for British governments after the war, but how quickly the surrounding picture had changed. At the end of World War II, a war that Britain and the Soviet Union had eventually fought as allies, the balance of national power had shifted irretrievably against Britain. The biggest question confronting an impoverished Britain's new Labor government in 1945 was what part it would play in the peace. Although the cost had been tremendous, Britain had earned a place at the victors' conference table. To all outward appearance, it was still a colonial power with interests and possessions to defend around the globe. Yet economically the Britain of 1945 was but a hollow shell of the imperial power it had once been.

It was all rather ironic. Britain had ended this war, unlike World War I, with no territorial claims on anyone. But the ruinous fight, plus the rapid termination of American Lend-Lease assistance, had left the country in straitened circumstances. The empire was no longer an asset and an expression of British power, but rather a barely supportable burden.

What is more, the world in which Britain operated had also changed. Once one of the great powers that settled the fate of nations, Britain emerged from the war, whether it understood it clearly at the time or not, dependent for future influence on the support of one or the other of the bigger and stronger powers, the United States or the Soviet Union. There was never any doubt about which power Britain would turn to in its newly dependent state. Cultural and political affinity, ideology and economic interest all pointed to alliance with the United States, just as ideological distaste, historical animosity, and Soviet actions in Europe immediately after the war dictated the search for security against the Soviet Union. The special relationship with America thus served two purposes for Britain. It helped Britain to hang on to at least the vestiges of a wider world role—albeit by clinging to the coattails of the American superpower—and thus perpetuated British influence longer than Britain's own reduced circumstances would otherwise have warranted. And it satisfied the need for safety in numbers in a world in which Britain could no longer expect to stand safely alone.

The choice was easy, but it was no less momentous for that. The search for security against Germany in the interwar years had turned in the postwar years into the search for security against the Soviet Union. That decision has been the cornerstone of every British government's foreign policy since the war. Whatever their ups and downs, it has also set the framework for Anglo-Soviet relations for the past forty years.

But choosing sides is only one element of foreign policy. From that decision flowed two others that have deeply affected British politics and Anglo-Soviet relations in the postwar period. First, there was Britain's commitment to a multilateral (not just a bilateral) military and political alliance structure in order to help contain any Soviet threat. Western Europe, to the extent that it managed to hang together, was seen by successive British governments as a secondary presence within this broader alliance. From a Soviet point of view, of course, this postwar alliance that has kept a well-armed America in Europe posed a direct threat to Soviet security and interests in Europe and elsewhere. To the extent that Britain worked hard for the establishment and maintenance of NATO, this was bound to sour future relations with Moscow.

The second decision was related to the first, though was not an inevitable consequence of it. That was the determination of each British government to date to maintain an independent nuclear deterrent—both for national defense and as a contribution to collective defense—and to provide basing facilities for American nuclear weapons in Europe.

All three postwar choices—for the special relationship with America, for NATO, and for nuclear weapons—flowed from an assessment shared broadly by both the government and opposition of the day that the Soviet Union was the chief threat. All three choices have profoundly affected the conduct of Anglo-Soviet relations. But from a Soviet point of view at least, it is the possession of an independent nuclear force that has always set Britain apart from the other European members of NATO. (France has nuclear weapons, too, but is no longer a member of the integrated military structure of the Alliance.) The Russians have always clearly understood the close link in British politics between security policy (meaning, above all, attitudes toward the Soviet Union) and the nuclear issue that was to surface in new form in the 1980s.

However, the choice of nuclear weapons as a part of Britain's defense forces was not based solely on their possible use as weapons. It was also a bid for continued influence in a world where influence was becoming a monopoly of the superpowers. It was the Labor government of Clement Attlee that first decided Britain should retain its independent nuclear deterrent. Aneurin Bevan's argument in 1957 to would-be unilateral disarmers inside his own party was that in the nuclear age the British foreign secretary could not go "naked into the conference chamber." As has been pointed out, he might have added that, without nuclear weapons, often Britain would not have been invited into the conference chamber at all.[3] In other words, the purpose of having nuclear weapons was both political and military. And indeed that purpose has been served. There is little doubt that possession of nuclear weapons has enabled Britain to play a larger part in world politics than it otherwise would have. The independent deterrent was in keeping with Britain's status as a permanent member of the United Nations security council and has kept Britain in close touch with the arms-control process. Like the special relationship with America, possession of the bomb has kept Britain more involved in the key issues of world power than a medium-sized European power might otherwise have expected.

Despite the efforts that went into containing and confronting the Soviet Union, the thread of pragmatism in Britain's dealings with the Soviet Union had not been lost. As one of the four wartime allies with continuing responsibilities for the peace in Europe, as a close ally of the United States, and as a nuclear weapons power, Britain saw its role in the 1950s and early 1960s as something of an "honest broker" in relations between the two opposing superpowers. The primary objective, through the Geneva conferences of 1955, the abortive Eisenhower-Khrushchev summit in 1960, and the not much more successful one between Kennedy and Khrushchev in 1961, was to keep open lines of communication as a way of containing the conflict between East and West to diplomatic and political channels.

This diplomatic dimension to Britain's security policy is a recurring theme in Anglo-American-Soviet relations since the war. During Soviet Prime Minister Alexei Kosygin's visit to London in 1967, Harold Wilson made a similar but unsuccessful effort to mediate via the Soviet Union between America and North Vietnam in the escalating war in South-East Asia.[4] In the 1980s, rather like Harold Macmillan in the late 1950s and early 1960s, Mrs. Thatcher has used her close relationship with President Reagan and her own increasing personal authority in foreign affairs both to help mitigate the conflicts that have arisen between the two superpowers and to convey to the Soviet Union the strength of Western determination not to allow Alliance differences to be exploited by the Kremlin.

The trouble with using one's good office to bring larger, opposing powers to the negotiation table is that once they are there summitry becomes a natural monopoly of the superpowers. In the 1960s Britain rapidly became preoccupied with its own search for a new political role in Europe as the trappings and powers of empire fell away. When it came to East-West relations its pragmatic approach was soon overshadowed, first in the 1960s by de Gaulle's vision of a Europe "from the Atlantic to the Urals" (a definition of Europe and of future East-West relations on the continent that seemed perfectly designed to minimize the Anglo-Saxon domination of the Western side), and then in the 1970s by West Germany's *Ostpolitik*.

The Soviet Union and Britain's Ostpolitik in the 1970s

Britain had participated in the gathering détente of the 1970s as an interested observer and a loyal member of the Western Alliance rather than as a leading player. Unlike the United States, which had great matters of strategic rivalry and arms control to settle with the Soviet Union, and unlike West Germany, which saw that the route to improved relations between the Germanies led initially through Moscow, Britain had no great political, emotional, or, indeed, economic stake in the outcome of détente. What Britain saw in the process was an opportunity to make relations with the West's chief adversary more stable and more calculable.

Thus, as tensions abated and East-West relations entered what Richard Nixon called the "era of negotiation," successive British governments were happy enough to cooperate in the multilateral discussions—at Vienna and Helsinki—that *Ostpolitik* brought in its wake. As one of the four powers with continuing responsibilities for Germany, Britain had a more prominent role, inevitably, in the negotiations that led to the four-power Berlin agreement in 1971. But otherwise its role was essentially a supportive one, if at times a valuable one for all that. And it was a role very much in the pragmatic tradition of British diplomacy. Of course, bilateral relations with the Soviet Union continued. But with East and West engaged across a broad front of military, political, economic, and cultural diplomacy, it made sense for Britain to pursue its goals in relations with the Soviet Union through a multilateral framework.

Nor, in the heavy days of summitry and *Ostpolitik* was Britain likely to loom large in Soviet calculations, except as a member of NATO and as a potential future problem in arms control. In any case, in the early

1970s Anglo-Soviet relations had the bloom knocked off them by the row that followed the expulsion of about a hundred Soviet diplomats from Britain for spying. (Although a loyal British subject and therefore unable so far to read the book *Spycatcher* by Peter Wright, the author is reliably informed of occasions when requests from the intelligence community that persons be expelled in this way were turned down so as not to damage Anglo-Soviet relations further.) With Harold Wilson's visit to Moscow in 1975, the Labor government had made efforts to improve relations. Wilson used the visit to announce a £950m credit at favorable rates in an attempt to stimulate trade. But the momentum generated was not great. The Soviet Union by this time had much larger fish to fry. By the time the credit agreement expired in 1980, the Soviet Union had used only £55m of it. Academic and cultural relations suffered for some considerable time as a result of the spying row and the cooling of relations, and were only just beginning to revive when the Soviet invasion of Afghanistan in December 1979 blighted relations once again.

The low-key, rather unemotional, nature of Britain's relations with the Soviet Union and expectations of East-West détente in the 1970s left Britain perhaps the least disappointed of the Western Allies when détente collapsed. With less national interest and ego invested in the outcome, and a natural skepticism about the grand designs for resolving East-West differences that were apt to appeal more to its European neighbors, Britain anyway had suitably modest expectations of what the détente of the 1970s could achieve. Indeed, from a British diplomatic point of view, the one pleasant surprise to emerge from the "decade of détente" was that the Helsinki agreement had proved to be a useful basis for nagging the Soviet Union about its human rights record, rather than just a piece of diplomatic confetti and a de facto recognition of Soviet control in Eastern Europe, as some had feared. All the same, despite the continued concern for human rights in both Eastern Europe and the Soviet Union, both Labor and Conservative governments in Britain in the 1970s had seemed to see détente as an implied acceptance of the territorial status quo in Europe and a contribution to stability there. They certainly had no desire openly to challenge the Soviet position in Eastern Europe, even if there were hopes that eventually the political and military bonds linking the Soviet Union and its East European allies would be loosened.

The Anglo-American-Soviet Triangle in the 1980s

Oddly, it was this rather pragmatic, unexcitable approach to relations with the Soviet Union and East-West relations in general that was to cause occasional ruffles in Anglo-American relations as the détente of the 1970s gave way to the angry rhetoric of the early 1980s. Yet the reasons have to do not just with temperament—after all, for a time the Thatcher government seemed to echo the hard anti-Soviet words of the new Reagan administration in the United States. They also have to do with geography and political preoccupation. While in many ways the Britain of the Thatcher government was the closest to, and most anxious to cooperate with, America in its condemnation of Soviet aggression in Afghanistan in 1979 and pressure on Poland in 1980–1981, Britain had not been entirely immune to all of the consequences of détente in Europe and its own political readjustment of focus to the horizons of the European communists in the West.

As Britain had adjusted more comfortably to its role as a medium-sized European power, it had come to see the Soviet Union increasingly, although by no means exclusively, in regional, that is European, terms. While Britain did not necessarily share the tendency of some of its partners in Europe to see détente as wholly divisible, regular political contact made Britain more aware of European, especially West German, sentiment and interests. And, despite Afghanistan, East-West relations in Europe had remained relatively stable. Although anxious to preserve the Atlantic Alliance as the cornerstone, if not the entire edifice, of British and West European security policy, Britain was still conscious of different European and American perspectives on the value of détente. She therefore found herself on several occasions trying to maintain a bridge between American and European policy as opinions differed on how to cope with Soviet actions outside Europe.

There was a growing feeling, too, in Britain and elsewhere in Europe, that after Afghanistan and Poland, however objectionable Soviet behavior, superpower relations were chilling too rapidly. Partly under the influence of Lord Carrington, until 1983 Britain's foreign secretary, Mrs. Thatcher appeared to tone down her own anti-Soviet rhetoric. "Megaphone diplomacy," as Lord Carrington had described it, gave way to a more measured approach to East-West relations and relations with the Soviet Union in particular. At least from 1983, Mrs. Thatcher made a deliberate bid for an improvement in East-West relations, beginning first with Eastern Europe, but also including the Soviet Union.

As a superpower, however, the United States saw its continuing rivalry with the Soviet Union in global terms. The invasion of Afghanistan, as well as the later Polish crisis, was interpreted by the later Carter administration and the subsequent Reagan administration in this global framework as a direct challenge to American and Western interests.[5] American pressure on its European allies to impose sanctions on the Soviet Union for its unacceptable behavior resulted in a series of disputes in U.S.–European relations in the early 1980s, which included Britain, albeit to a lesser extent than West Germany.

Although in many cases, such as the boycott of the 1980 Moscow Olympics, the British government sided with the United States, the impression left was that this was done despite sometimes differing views about the efficacy of sanctions. Because of its traditionally close ties to the United States, because of the warm personal regard between Thatcher and Reagan, and again because the Thatcher government continued to see Western solidarity as the cornerstone of its security policy, Britain had not sought to make public such differences.

Yet some have inevitably shown through. American attempts in the early 1980s to block European trade with the Soviet Union and prevent European equipment from going to help build a Soviet gas pipeline to Western Europe were deeply resented throughout Europe, including in Britain. In this case the Thatcher government took measures to ensure that British companies' did not lose out for political reasons in the competition with other European companies for contracts on the pipeline. The trans-Atlantic rancor on this issue was compounded in Britain, as elsewhere in Europe, by President Reagan's refusal to block U.S. grain sales to the Soviet Union while trying to stop European sales of machinery.

President Reagan's SDI program is another case in which the British government has not seen eye-to-eye with its chief ally. The difference is not so much about the nature of the Soviet threat as about how to cope with it. Although Britain has agreed to cooperate in the SDI research program, and some firms and universities have accepted SDI-related contracts, within parts of the British government there is considerable skepticism, not just about the feasibility of space-based defenses but also about their desirability. The reasons are several.

As a nuclear power itself, Britain, like France and China, is worried that its own nuclear deterrent would be devalued by any Soviet decision to match future American deployment of an SDI system. There is concern, too, that SDI will either trigger such a weapons race in space or encourage the Soviet Union to expand its own nuclear arsenal in an effort to defeat SDI. Either way, the argument runs, the result would destabilize the nuclear balance and defeat long-standing attempts to introduce greater calculability into the East-West military relationship. Sir Geoffrey Howe, the British foreign secretary, expressed some of those fears in a speech to the Royal United Services Institute in London in 1985, when he warned SDI's promoters of the dangers of creating "a Maginot line in space."

The British prime minister may not have shared all her foreign secretary's reservations about SDI, and for reasons of Alliance solidarity on the crucial issue of security has anyway not wished to differ openly with President Reagan on this issue. All the same, in 1984 she extracted from the president a set of principles that she believes limits the present SDI effort to research on the relevant technologies and commits the American government to consultations before any future deployment takes place. She took further ideas with her to Moscow in the spring of 1987, in an apparent attempt to break the stalemate in U.S.–Soviet discussions of SDI and raised them again in her brief talks with Mikhail Gorbachev when he stopped over for a few hours at Britain's Brize Norton air base on his way to the Washington summit in December. Although the American government was aware of what she planned to say to Mr. Gorbachev, it was clear that Mrs. Thatcher does not completely share President Reagan's faith in SDI. Although SDI is seen by the British government as a part of the new U.S. resolve that brought the Soviets back to the negotiating table at Geneva, its value is seen more as a bargaining chip—to be cashed in at some point for an agreement on strategic nuclear weapons—rather than as something either desirable in its own right or to be used to demonstrate Western technological or economic superiority.

SDI is an important issue for Britain because of its obvious link to security and defense policy. The INF treaty abolishing American and Soviet land-based missiles in Europe with ranges between 500–5000 kilometers presents something of a similar problem. Britain backed President Reagan's "zero option" as a political gambit to win the public relations battle with the Soviet Union over arms control during the debate over deployment of American cruise and Pershing-2 missiles in Europe. Yet there was no disguising the dismay felt by some British government officials after the Reykjavik summit, at which President Reagan appeared to connive with Gorbachev in the rhetoric of a "postnuclear" world. (The reaction caused some surprise in Moscow, where European unease about SDI had led to exaggerated expectations of the possibilities for splitting the Western allies from America in rather different ways.)

Similarly, when zero-zero eventually became double-zero (with the decision to include missiles with ranges down to 500km, not just the original medium-range missiles), there was concern that in the pursuit of a deal on medium-range nuclear weapons in Europe, the United States would begin a process that would end with the unraveling of nuclear deterrence, the cornerstone of NATO strategy for the defense of Europe. Had the British government not been about to embark on a general election at the time, in spring 1987, these reservations might have been more publicly expressed. As is argued below, however, the government did not want to go into an election critical of the first superpower arms control deal for more than a decade.

There was also another problem to be reckoned with, that of maintaining the cohesion and bargaining strength of the Western Alliance during a period of weakness and indecision in Washington in the wake of the Irangate affair. Mrs. Thatcher shared with several of her fellow European prime ministers a worry that an obvious weakening of American leadership in the Western Alliance could have serious consequences for Alliance cohesion at a time when the Soviet Union was being led by a more sophisticated and more intelligent general secretary than any since the war. Both because of her own regard for the American president and because of these wider worries about coping with a new Soviet charm offensive at a time of American weakness, Mrs. Thatcher sought to emphasize her public solidarity with the president, despite differences over important details of policy.

Does all this new activity on the part of the British government add up to a special role for Britain in East-West relations? Indeed, does it presage a revival of the sort of global foreign policy that Britain tried to carry out before the withdrawal from East of Suez?

There is little doubt that during the 1980s changes occurred in British politics and policy that opened up new possibilities in foreign policy. Of course, some things had not changed: Britain was still a nuclear power, was still a member of the U.N. Security Council, and still had a reasonably close relationship with America. It was not what might be called these "permanently operating factors" that offered greater scope for British diplomacy in the 1980s, but the less tangible, more transient ones of personality, economic performance, and political opportunity.

Margaret Thatcher is now the longest-serving British prime minister of the century and a forceful one at that. She has been in power since 1979, through the downs and more recent ups of the last decade of East-West relations. It therefore becomes hard to separate the personality of the prime minister from the intellectual drive behind her policies. Few British prime ministers since the war have left such a deep personal imprint on national policy. None since the 1950s has been as successful in exploiting British national assets to diplomatic effect on the wider world stage. There is little doubt that outside events—the unpleasant shock of the Falklands War in 1982 and the seemingly unstoppable slide in superpower relations in the early 1980s—would have propelled even the most hesitant of British prime ministers to take an interest in foreign affairs. Whatever else her critics have said about her, none has ever accused Mrs. Thatcher of reluctance to put her own guiding hand on the policy tiller. When the prime minister decided in 1983 to take a more active role abroad, especially in East-West relations, she has done so with a deliberation that has characterized other changes of the Thatcher years. Academic and other outside advisers were consulted in addition to her own Foreign Office, differing views canvassed and then the diplomatic machinery cranked into action.

Of course, it helped enormously that to critical outside eyes, including in the Kremlin, Britain's economic troubles of the 1970s were being tackled at home with a will, if not always with a consensus. In the 1970s it was said of the Wilson and Callaghan governments that the weakness of British foreign policy was the weakness of the British economy. Certainly, in the 1980s, the return to growth at home has been matched by a return to new-found respect and influence abroad. Yet precisely because of the forceful personality of the prime minister, this shift in Britain's diplomatic fortunes is bound to be seen in large part as the work of a single, remarkable leader rather than as a more fundamental shift in Britain's role as a medium-sized European power, albeit one with some interesting historical connections through former empire and present-day Commonwealth and with a reservoir of diplomatic expertise.

Nor, against this background, is it surprising that, so far at least, the thrust of this new Thatcher-charged foreign policy has propelled Britain into a more prominent role in East-West relations. This was not only the traditional concern of British governments from Attlee on, it also happened to be the arena in the 1980s in which political opportunity conspired with economic performance and the personality of the British prime minister of the day to expand, at least temporarily, the role Britain was able to play. Partly because other European countries were temporarily out of the running (West Germany was being cold-shouldered by the Russians for deploying new NATO missiles; France's President Mitterrand was not the favorite in Moscow that some of his predecessors had been), partly because of

Mrs. Thatcher's close ties with President Reagan, Britain had the opportunity in the mid-1980s to play a larger part in East-West relations than it has been inclined or able to do for some time. Add to that a genuinely good personal relationship with Mikhail Gorbachev and Mrs. Thatcher's considerable experience in foreign affairs at a time when America was seen to be weakened by domestic scandals and the opportunity widened still further.

The revival of Britain's *Ostpolitik*, personified in Mrs. Thatcher's visit to Moscow in spring 1987, has to be seen against this background. This was not an act of incipient British Gaullism, seeking to carve out an independent role for Britain in a new Europe. In fact it was very much in the tradition of postwar British diplomacy, seeking to enhance the security of Britain and its major allies by bringing some greater calculability to the relationship with its chief adversary. The British prime minister was not acting as messenger or go-between; the superpowers were already doing their own talking. But while she was able to dispel any misconceptions in Moscow about Western cohesion over security policy, she was also able to represent a reasoned European voice in Moscow at a critical time in East-West relations.

As for the British government's attitude to the changes in Moscow under Gorbachev and their consequences for East-West relations, this was summed up in typically cautious and pragmatic style by Sir Geoffrey Howe as "realism, vigilance and an open mind."[6] The problems that come with the differences of ideology, politics, and interests that have dogged Anglo-Soviet relations since the war are not expected to dissolve, even with a more sophisticated and open-minded leader in the Kremlin. Nor is there a particularly momentous bilateral agenda of issues, as distinct from the shared security and human rights concerns of the Western Alliance, to be pursued in Moscow. Indeed, the prime minister's open admiration for Gorbachev's courage in pursuing reform is not matched in official Foreign Office or government circles by blindness, either to the Soviet Union's continuing poor human rights record or to the political and military differences that make the Soviet Union a difficult country to live with. Nor is there any great enthusiasm for including the Soviet Union in the outside world's international economic organizations, like the GATT and the IMF. And for the foreseeable future, the British government will remain acutely wary of anything that smacks of a grand design for remolding European politics, whether the impulse for such a new design comes from East or West. The preferred response to the Gorbachev phenomenon under the Thatcher government is to respond to greater sophistication on the Soviet side with better thought-out policies from the West, not with accommodation to the new Soviet regime.

Britain's Domestic Debate

It did no harm at all in Britain, or elsewhere in Western Europe, in the changing political climate in the 1980s to see a tough, pronuclear prime minister being treated by Moscow as a political weight to be reckoned with. The importance of Mrs. Thatcher's developing relationship with the new Soviet leader lies not just in its foreign policy purposes, but also in its implications for Britain's domestic debate about those old issues of alliance, security, and attitudes to the two superpowers.

There is no doubt that in the past, especially in the 1920s and 1930s, attitudes toward the Soviet Union have played a role in British domestic politics. There was much sympathy in those years on the left of British politics for the fledgling Soviet state.[7] Even after World War II, some intellectuals found the transition in British official attitudes to the Soviet Union—from wartime ally to peacetime foe—hard to swallow: a problem that gave rise to some of the most damaging espionage cases involving British intelligence in the postwar years. And Britain has its share of revisionist histories of the Cold War period.[8]

However, for most of the left, the Stalin purges of the 1930s and Soviet actions in the late 1940s in Eastern Europe served to destroy sympathy for the Soviet regime. Thus, unlike in France or Italy, both of which had large Communist parties on the left of the political spectrum, in Britain, Soviet actions had ensured that the major left-wing party was opposed to Soviet policy in Europe. To the extent that the Soviet Union was a polarizing factor in British politics in the 1950s, at the parliamentary level at least it meant that the few pro-Soviet voices were isolated in a tiny minority of the Labor fringe. For all practical purposes, the Soviet Union had little impact on British domestic politics, once the major postwar foreign policy choices had been made.

As far as public opinion in general about the Soviet Union was concerned, there seemed to be little of it. Until the early 1980s, foreign policy issues seldom held the attention of the British public for long. To the extent that attitudes to the Soviet Union could be divined, these were enduringly hostile.[9] Of course, public opinion is seldom either simple to analyze or stable for long. Although the Soviet Union is not a country that is always at the forefront of public attention in Britain, the British public has not been altogether uninterested in the Soviet

Union. On the contrary, when Khrushchev and Bulganin visited Britain in 1956, there was enormous media and public interest, just as there was when the Soviet Union launched Sputnik, when it put the first man in space, and on similar occasions since. But public interest in newsworthy events is inevitably intermittent. For the most part, while Britons have been prepared to gawk at visiting Soviet leaders as something of a rarity and to admire spectacular scientific achievements, the Soviet Union is more routinely seen as a not very attractive place that has pursued an often hostile foreign policy, which is held in check, at least in Europe, by the Western Alliance. The Soviet Union is therefore seen as a legitimate matter of government concern, but not as a burning issue of public debate. When the Soviet Union does something hostile, such as invading Afghanistan, this is seen as less remarkable only because it is a country that the British have come to expect to behave badly.

Not that there has been no change in British attitudes to the Soviet threat over the years. The old Communist menace on the domestic scene—whether imagined or real—is no longer a feature of British politics. That has compounded the apparent indifference of British public opinion toward the Soviet Union. Similarly, the external threat posed by the Soviet Union has been seen to change through the era of negotiation in the late 1960s and early 1970s, and despite Soviet bad behavior in the early 1980s. Partly because of NATO's success in keeping the European peace for the past forty years, partly because the ideological force of communism has waned around the globe, the Soviet Union is perceived these days as a more ordinary superpower. Though still a potential threat, it no longer seems poised to lurch for the Channel—the old image of the red stain spreading across free Europe. Nuclear accidents aside, these days Britons, like other West Europeans, are more likely to worry about how the Soviet Union might react to crises elsewhere—in Eastern Europe, the Middle East, the Persian Gulf. But crises such as these have so far generally been managed between the major powers rather than taken as causes for immediate hostilities. In other words, the worry is that miscalculation might lead East or West into a conflict that neither side really wants. That is still a rather more remote threat than worrying about the enemy tank barrels lined up at the NATO–Warsaw Pact frontier in the heart of Europe, even though the threat of Soviet military power remains.[10]

Yet, there is no doubt that, like elsewhere in Western Europe, public opinion in Britain in the early 1980s was, comparatively speaking, seething. The question is: with what? Not, it seems, with a change of attitude toward the Soviet Union. On the contrary, although there has been considerable recent interest in Gorbachev as an individual (no doubt helped by the good reference he received when Mrs. Thatcher proclaimed: "We can do business with him"), there has still been no noticeable change in British attitudes to the Soviet Union itself and the threat it poses to Western security. This may change if *glasnost* results in a more humane human rights policy in the Soviet Union and if reform brings fundamental change to Soviet society. But so far at least, the Gorbachev effect on British attitudes toward the Soviet Union has yet to overcome the "Gulag effect."

But if attitudes to the Soviet Union are hard to shift, the same is not true of attitudes toward Britain's chief ally, the United States, and those perennial issues of defense and nuclear weapons. Opinion polls began registering public concern over both American leadership and the nuclear weapons issue in the early 1980s. However, the reasons for this shift are not as straightforward as might be assumed.

The first change was a major breakdown of the consensus within Britain between the major political parties on defense that had endured since the end of the war. Following the Labor party's defeat in the 1979 election, there was a major shift within the party away from the traditional pro-Atlanticist support for NATO's nuclear weapons policy. The Labor party as a whole had always been divided on defense. Hugh Gaitskill had been defeated at the party's conference in 1962 on the issue of unilateral disarmament; Wilson, in opposition, had been critical of the original decision by the Macmillan government to buy the Polaris submarine from the United States. Yet, once in office, Labor governments had consistently seen the logic of keeping an independent British nuclear deterrent and of maintaining bases for American nuclear weapons in Britain. In the 1980s, however, the Labor party chose two consecutive leaders in opposition—Michael Foot and Neil Kinnock—who are firmly antinuclear in their thinking and pro-unilateral disarmament in their politics. As a result, it can no longer be assumed by Britain's allies in NATO that a future Labor government would follow the pattern of being antinuclear in opposition but pronuclear in power.

Inevitably, the breakdown of the bipartisan consensus on defense and security policy has contributed to the reawakening of the nuclear debate in Britain—a debate that since the beginnings of the Campaign for Nuclear Disarmament (CND) in the 1950s had been remarkable for the most part only by its absence. But the effect of this resurgent defense debate was magnified by an almost coincidental event: the plan to deploy new American cruise missiles in Europe, including in

Britain, to counter the Soviet SS-20s. Although Britain's original support for NATO's decision to counter the SS-20s if negotiations failed came from a Labor government, the rift between (and in Labor's case within) the political parties polarized the public debate on this issue. The row over defense was serious enough to lead to a formal split within the Labor party and was one of the reasons for the creation of the Social Democratic Party (SDP).

The defense row also happened to coincide in Britain in particular with a program of major public spending cuts introduced by the Thatcher government. Defense and nuclear weapons were largely exempted from the cuts. Defense policy, as embodied by the Trident replacement for Polaris, could be, and indeed was, portrayed by the Labor opposition as taking funds away from social programs, such as health and education. As has been pointed out elsewhere, a radical Conservative government combined with a radical Labor opposition to further polarize the defense debate.[11]

The impact of all this political turmoil on public opinion was noticeable. But it was also clear that the turmoil resulted from changes in British domestic politics and within the two major political parties. It was driven by domestic issues, even though it had potentially important implications for foreign policy. That may be one important reason that, for all the street marches and peace camps of the early 1980s, the nuclear issue did not have the enduring political impact that it perhaps ought to have had.

Partly because of Labor's own internal divisions on defense, partly because the party misread the real public mood, and partly because of the intervening "Falklands factor" (the Falklands war of 1982 made many Britons acutely aware of the need for sound defense—albeit in support of interests far from the British mainland), the general election of 1983 returned the pro-NATO, pronuclear Thatcher government to power with a thumping majority. Subsequent analysis of the "missile debate" in Britain, and indeed elsewhere in Europe, has shown that the issue arose not because of any fundamental shift in attitudes toward the Soviet Union, nor toward NATO, nor toward nuclear weapons as such. In Britain, American nuclear weapons are probably less popular than they used to be, but mainly because Britons suddenly had to focus on their existence for the first time in many years. Britain's own nuclear weapons are less unpopular, and even during the missile debate, opinion polls continued to register high levels of support for them. If the issue was not therefore what it seemed, what was it?

The cause of the public anxiety about defense and nuclear weapons would seem to be a feeling, exemplified by the arrival of the new missiles and compounded by the harsh anti-Soviet rhetoric of the early Reagan years, that superpower relations were sliding out of control. This would appear to be supported by the evidence that, once the superpowers resumed negotiations, the missile issue in Britain faded as fast as it had arisen.

Given the close postwar relationship between Britain's defense and security policy and assumptions about the Soviet threat, there was bound to be some implications in the defense debate for attitudes toward the Soviet Union, and some scope for an improvement in relations with the Soviet Union to feed back into the defense debate in the late 1980s and early 1990s. However, it is argued here that such a change, if it happened, would be the consequence of changes in public opinion, not their cause. And indeed, both the Soviet Union and defense played a role in the 1987 British election that provided Mrs. Thatcher with the opportunity to turn her period in office into what is bound to be seen as the Thatcher "era" in British politics.

Seldom since the war had the British public been offered such a clear choice on defense as it was in both the 1983 and 1987 elections: between pro-NATO, pronuclear Conservatives, and antinuclear, pro-unilateral disarmament Labor. Once again, in 1987, the defense issue rebounded on the Labor party, whose policy of "defensive deterrence" (getting rid of both British and American nuclear weapons) was lampooned by Labor's opponents as "defenseless defense." Newspaper advertisements placed by the Conservative party in the weeks before the election showed a petite young lady in smudged makeup and camouflage uniform surrendering to the unnamed foe. The nature of the enemy could be seen from Conservative political broadcasts on television that showed a map of Europe, its eastern half in lurid red. If the picture seemed a little crude, especially just a few weeks after Mrs. Thatcher had stood beaming next to Mr. Gorbachev at the Bolshoi ballet, it perhaps showed how easy it still was in Britain to tap the old images of the Soviet Union. Denis Healey, a former Labor defense minster and member of the shadow cabinet (and a pronuclear man in his government days), did neither himself nor his party much good by saying, after a trip to Moscow hard on Mrs. Thatcher's heels, that the Soviets were "praying for a Labor victory." Few wavering Britons were likely to be persuaded to vote for a party that felt it needed this sort of endorsement.

Yet for all the symbolism and use by both Labor and Conservative parties of the Soviet connection to put over their different cases, it was hard to avoid the impression that both were using their preferred images of the Soviet Union to sell their particular brand of defense policy, rather than raising the more fundamental issue of whether the role of the Soviet Union in British foreign and security policy was really changing. The question was not so much whether the Soviet Union was still a threat, but what type of threat it could be said to pose—and therefore what type of defense policy could be sold to the public. After all, the defense debate in Britain had pre-dated Mr. Gorbachev by several years. It was not sparked by him.

Put in crude terms, the Labor party wanted to abolish Britain's nuclear role and so argued that it was not in Soviet interests to attack Britain. Commitment to unilateral disarmament is often as much an act of faith and a statement of moral interpretation as the outcome of a rational political assessment of Britain's changing external security environment. The Conservative party, wanting to uphold Britain's nuclear role, argued instead the old case for a Soviet threat to British security, despite changes in Moscow. It was all good political theater, but it said little about the future of Anglo-Soviet relations under either party. The majority of the British public, reassured by the general warmth of East-West relations, appeared to assume that all was well enough and voted as they had done at previous elections, according to what they saw as their own economic interests—and in the process ensured that Thatcherism in foreign policy, as well as at home, would endure into the 1990s.

Fault Lines in the Alliance in the 1990s

Mrs. Thatcher is very much a traditionalist politician abroad despite her revisionism at home. The new activism in British foreign policy in the 1980s has been in defense of traditional postwar values: security, Alliance, and nuclear deterrence. Yet it would be wrong to leave the impression that attitudes to the Soviet Union in Britain are unchanging and unchangeable.

There have been a number of polls in recent years, even before Mr. Gorbachev came to power, that have shown the Soviet leader of the day ranked not very far behind President Reagan in contribution to peace, leadership qualities, and so on—but only because President Reagan has at times sunk close to the habitual Soviet level. Britons, like other Europeans, have often reacted in worried fashion, first to the harsh anti-Soviet rhetoric of the early Reagan years and later to unilateral actions on the part of America, such as the bombing raid on Libya. But what many people in the U.S. have seen as a rise in anti-Americanism in Britain is really an "antisuperpowerism." The British have shown little faith in American leadership under President Reagan.

But opinion polls showing his popularity sinking lower than that of Mr. Gorbachev should not be taken as indicating a "moral equivalence" between the two superpowers. Naturally enough, allies tend to be held to higher standards than adversaries. When asked about America and the Soviet Union as countries and people, the picture the polls draw is radically different.

All this suggests that a different president could turn the approval ratings around. The chief conclusion to be drawn is that an American president has far more scope than a Soviet party leader to affect public opinion in Britain. Any American administration in the 1990s will be held up to more detailed examination than the Kremlin. Thus, what happens in the U.S. elections is more likely to affect British public attitudes than what happens in East-West relations, provided the latter remains reasonably stable.

A second conclusion flows from this: namely, that the issue of British defense policy, to the extent that it remains a matter of public debate into the 1990s, is also more likely to be affected by developments within NATO than directly by Soviet actions. This could have difficult consequences for Anglo-American relations if differences widen, either over SDI or what follows from an INF agreement. One issue that could cause problems, for example, is the degree to which an INF agreement is seen to impinge on British sovereignty over bases where American weapons are housed. Verifications procedures agreed upon between America and the Soviet Union will apply to British sovereign territory as well.

But there is also a much bigger issue looming in American-European relations: that of the role of nuclear weapons in NATO strategy. To the extent that the impulse at Reykjavik toward a "nuclear-free" world represents a real shift in American strategic thinking, then a rift is bound to open between America and its allies in Europe. Geography dictates that, in case of war, nuclear weapons are the chief threat to the American homeland. The propaganda in support of SDI, emphasizing the ability to shield America (though in practice probably only America's own missiles) from Soviet nuclear attack, reflects this perception of where the chief threat to American security comes from. To many Europeans, however, faced with huge Soviet conventional forces in Europe, nuclear weapons are a vital element in NATO strategy for deterring a Soviet attack in Europe. Any attempt to downplay the role of nuclear weapons is therefore bound to raise fears that NATO's defense will unravel too. And this time the worry about American strategy is not confined to the protest marchers; it is widely shared in government circles.

In the near term, under the Thatcher government, the consequences of such divergent opinions will be contained in the case of Britain by the continued commitment to the three pillars of postwar British security policy: friendship with America, membership in NATO, and vocal support for nuclear deterrence. The latter could, however, become a problem if at some point in the future Britain is put under pressure to abandon its own nuclear weapons in the interests of a superpower arms control agreement that it feels does not adequately safeguard British and European security. Britain, unlike France, has said that at some point Britain's nuclear weapons could become part of the arms reduction process, but there is little enthusiasm for the idea and the point is felt to be very far in the future.

Under any other government, whether Labor, post-Thatcher Conservative, or coalition, the picture is bound to change. The Labor party, under its present leader and with its present policies, would have to contemplate a major rift, not just with America but also with its European allies. The impact of a British abandonment of nuclear weapons on a unilateral basis would have profound implications for NATO. But the commitment by Labor to abandon nuclear weapons was made before Gorbachev came to power and would, if upheld in its original form, be carried out irrespective of changes for better or worse in Soviet foreign policy or Britain's external security. However, following Labor's second heavy defeat in a row, the 1987 election did produce the beginnings of a rethinking of policy, designed to produce more attractive and electable policies for the 1990s. The argument that Labor is unelectable with its unilateralist defense policy has gained currency within some sections of the party's leadership. However, the shape of any future compromise is still unclear. If the party settles on a policy of abandoning Britain's nuclear deterrent unilaterally while staying within a nuclear-armed NATO, the confusion could well leave Labor no better off at the polling booths. Labor strategists are therefore hoping that by the time of the next British election, possibly not until 1992, the superpower arms control process will have removed the problem for them—by leaving Mrs. Thatcher or whoever succeeds her as leader of the Conservative party isolated in the commitment to a continued British deterrent.

Looking farther ahead than the next British general election, the picture becomes even cloudier. The shift toward Europe within all political parties, in political, economic, and defense terms, could put extra strain on Anglo-American relations. Witness the row in the Conservative party in 1986 over whether Britain's Westland helicopter company should be taken over by an American company or a

European consortium. It led to the resignation of the defense secretary, Michael Heseltine, when the decision went against the Europeans.

Despite Mrs. Thatcher's personal commitment to it, the special relationship with the U.S. is not what it was. Distrust of American policy and political leadership has increased greater European cooperation on defense. This began, especially within the SDP, as a way of shoring up the European pillar of NATO and reducing European-American friction over the burden of defense. But unless carefully handled on both sides of the Atlantic, the issue could become divisive. Just as the superpowers are criticized in Europe, whether they get too friendly or fall out too seriously, so also Europeans sometimes feel they cannot win. If they organize themselves better for European defense, they are sometimes seen as a challenge by the U.S.; if they cooperate less among themselves, they are criticized for doing too little.

However, the pressure for greater European defense cooperation now seems irresistible, whether or not the United States maintains as many troops on the ground in Europe ten years from now as it does today. Defense cooperation is generally viewed as a good thing. However, the process of achieving more of it in Europe and the forms it might take in the wake of the INF agreement are already causing concern. One issue that will prove particularly difficult in the wake of INF is the planned modernization of NATO's short-range nuclear weapons, especially those in West Germany. Neither Britain nor France shares West Germany's apparent interest in seeing these weapons either removed or allowed to become obsolete.

Add to all of this the "Gorbachev factor," meaning not just the smiling face of the new Soviet leader but also the Soviet propensity since 1985 for scattering new arms proposals like so much confetti, and the possibilities for playing on the natural fault lines in the Western Alliance are bound to increase over the coming decade. Precisely by virtue of the weight and self-confidence that has returned to British foreign policy in the late 1980s, Britain will have an important part to play in shaping Western policy and the Western response to Soviet initiatives. How will Britain respond? Of course, much will depend on who governs Britain, its major allies, especially America, and the Soviet Union in the 1990s. Yet there are some pointers to the future from the trends evident in the 1980s.

Despite talk of a new era in East-West relations—even of a "post-Yalta" framework for Europe—successive British governments have always been skeptical of grand designs and quietly in favor of the status quo. Mrs. Thatcher differs only in the extent that she has talked more openly of defense of traditional values in security policy and

East-West relations. Thus far at least, the official view in Britain has been that if barriers are to be removed in Europe, the onus is on the East to remove those that it has put in the way of the free flow of information and people. Security barriers ought to be the last to go, not the first. There has traditionally been little patience, if any, for attempts to use arms control to redraw the political map of Europe, a tendency most marked on the far left fringes of West German politics.

Thus far, too, Britain has remained officially committed both to maintaining an independent British nuclear deterrent and to nuclear weapons as a central pillar of NATO security policy. Indeed, Mrs. Thatcher has never been more assiduous in her determination to keep talking to and persuading official Washington than when talk surfaces in the White House about a "nuclear-free" world. Even the Labor party, under pressure from public opinion as expressed through the ballot box, has been forced to rethink its total opposition to nuclear defense. However, this is one area where a change of government in the 1990s could still bring major changes to British security policy.

Yet despite Labor's ambivalence about nuclear issues, neither of the two major political parties in Britain has yet shown real signs of being carried away by talk of a "Europeanization of Europe," a phrase that emerged on the semineutralist European left during the missile debate of the early 1980s and denoted the exclusion of both superpowers from Europe. The idea has since been coopted by the Soviet Union under the guise of what it refers to as the "common European house," in an attempt to exclude America. Neither version has had much appeal in the mainstream of British politics. However CND, robbed of some of its antinuclear thunder by the INF agreement, has already begun to give rein to its anti-American instincts implicit in earlier campaigns.

There is little support in Britain for fiddling with the postwar settlement in Europe. There has always been considerable sympathy for the postwar plight of Eastern Europe when events have focused media attention on it. But to most Britons, most of the time, Europe means Western Europe. There has certainly never been a strong cultural or political affinity with the Slavic nations of Eastern Europe. Nor, more than forty years after the war, has there been any significant domestic pressure on British governments to intervene in Eastern Europe when crises have occurred. It is unlikely that future British governments of whatever complexion will feel pressed to make compromises in foreign policy either to encourage or accommodate political change in Eastern Europe.

Yet while Britain is likely to remain the most skeptical of all the West European countries when it comes to talk of a "common

European house" and the like, there is still the question of Britain's future relations with the Soviet Union. As the 1980s draw to a close, Anglo-Soviet relations are at their warmest in several decades. Are there grounds for assuming that this relationship will endure? And, if so, what are the likely consequences for British policy? Will Mrs. Thatcher, or whoever succeeds her as prime minister and inherits the foreign policy she has established, be tempted to pursue a sort of British Gaullism, using improved relations with Moscow to carve out a high profile and a more idiosyncratic policy within the Western Alliance?

On the durability of improved Anglo-Soviet relations, there is little intrinsic reason to count on it. The conditions that conspired to offer Britain a wider role on this particular issue may change. France or West Germany may become the particular target of Soviet foreign policy in Europe, thereby relegating Britain more to the sidelines, as in the 1970s. The next American president or Soviet general secretary may be less inclined to listen to a British prime minister. And the next British prime minister may carry less personal influence than Mrs. Thatcher. The United Kingdom's new-found self-confidence may find alternative outlets on the world stage.

Yet even if the current mutual respect is preserved between British and American and between British and Soviet leaders of the future, this is unlikely to translate into uniquely British policy initiatives, except within the framework of Allied policy on East-West relations. Relations between Britain and the Soviet Union at the end of the 1980s, although undeniably warmer than in recent years, are still beset by the caution explained in the extract from the British parliamentary report cited earlier. Britain still has lingering memories of grating empires and fresher ones of the problems of living close to the Eurasian land mass with a large and powerful neighbor with very different interests and objectives.

Thus, Britain's agenda in relations with the Soviet Union remains very much the traditional one. Unless the Western Alliance fragments, or one of its members steps far beyond the consensus on security policy and East-West relations, Britain is likely to continue to see the Alliance framework as the best guarantee of its own security—and concentrate on helping the Alliance manage its relations with the Soviet Union, rather than attempt take over that management itself. With all the self-confidence in the world at its disposal, no future British government will have the military or political weight to stand alone. It cannot be ruled out entirely that a future British government of the left would decide to try to take Britain out of the security framework of the past forty years. It is not impossible, but it is unlikely. Even on the Labor left in Britain, there is a recognition that in political and military affairs, as in economic ones, Britain will do best as part of a similar-minded grouping. Whether that grouping remains the Atlantic Alliance as understood for the past decades or some new Eurocentered group depends less on the future course of Anglo-Soviet relations than on how well the Alliance manages its own internal differences in the 1990s.

Notes

1. UK-Soviet Relations. Second Report from the Foreign Affairs Committee, House of Commons Paper 28-I, Vol. 1, 1986 p. xi.
2. "East-West Relations: The British Role," published in East-West Relations. Realism, Vigilance and Open Mind, prepared for the Foreign and Commonwealth Office by the Central Office of Information, 1987.
3. Edward Spiers, "The British Nuclear Deterrent: Problems and Possibilities," in David Dilks, ed., *Retreat From Power: Studies in Britain's Foreign Policy of the Twentieth Century, Vol. 2, After 1939* (London: Macmillan, 1981), p. 158.
4. G. Segal, *The Great Power Triangle* (London: Macmillan, 1982), chapter 4.
5. The contrast between European and American perspectives is argued out in Lawrence Freedman, "The United States Factor," in E. Moreton and G. Segal, eds., *Soviet Strategy Towards Western Europe* (London: Allen and Unwin, 1984).
6. "East-West Relations: The British Role," cited above.
7. See F. S. Northedge and Audrey Wells, *Britain and Soviet Communism. The Impact of a Revolution* (London: Macmillan 1982), chapters 6 and 7.
8. See, for example, A. J. P. Taylor, *Europe: Grandeur and Decline* (London: Pelican Books, 1967), especially the preface.
9. Ivor Crewe, "Britain: Two and a Half Cheers for the Atlantic Alliance," in Gregory Flynn and Hans Rattinger, eds., *The Public and Atlantic Defense* (London: Croom Helm, 1985), chapter 2, p. 15.
10. E. Moreton, "Images of the Soviet Union: A More Typical Adversary," in G. Flynn et al, *Public Images of Western Security*, Atlantic Papers, No. 54/55, pp. 16–35.
11. David Robertson and Robbin Laird, "The Future of British Defense Policy," (monograph, undated) p. 6–7.

The United States and the Soviet Union

Stanley Hoffmann

To write about American attitudes toward and relations with the Soviet Union is tantamount to writing about American foreign policy after World War II. The contest between the two principal winners of that war has provided the text and the rationale for America's performance on the world stage. For more than forty years, the guidelines of American diplomacy have been containment and coexistence: containment in order to limit the expansion of Soviet power and influence, coexistence because—even before nuclear parity—most Americans have wanted to prevent the superpowers' rivalry from leading to the catastrophe of another global war. This essay will focus on the foundations of American policy, the main features of the superpower relationship, the connections between policy toward the Soviet Union and domestic politics, the connections with NATO, and finally the future prospects.

Foundations

Many distinguished critics of American diplomacy in particular, and democratic foreign policy in general, have written about the discontinuity and pusillanimity of a political strategy that has to be defined openly while being subjected to all the vicissitudes of public opinion and partisan maneuvers. And yet, the proverbial observer from Mars—or the dispassionate historian—is more likely to be struck by the durability of the course that was devised in the crucial period 1946–1949. A recent attack on American moves in the Persian Gulf in 1987[1] shows how much they—or at least the rationalizations offered by officials—owe to the Truman doctrine of forty years ago. In other words, the foundations are deep and have proved exceptionally solid. Why?

"Realists" would answer that America's policy is simply rooted in reality. The Soviet Union and the United States emerged as the only major powers after the collapse of Europe and the capitulation of Japan. There were, of course, huge disparities in power between them; but even though the United States had a nuclear monopoly and enormous economic resources while the Soviet Union had suffered staggering losses and destruction, Moscow had important assets: a geographical position in the heartland that made Western Europe and much of Asia hostages to its armies, a philosophy of history, or ideology, that was geared to expansion, and a network of Communist parties and sympathizers in many parts of the world. Only the United States could establish and preserve a balance of power against the Soviet Union. It was therefore normal that the leading maritime power should forge a coalition with the threatened states on the European continent. It was also normal that this power should count on nuclear deterrence to prevent its rival from initiating not only nuclear war, once Moscow had broken the American monopoly, but also conventional war in strategically vital areas in which the Soviets enjoyed military advantages. It is easy to spin out an explanation based on the necessities of power of the sort Thucydides would have given—with Washington in the role of Sparta, moved by the fear of Soviet power.

However, this explanation assumes that states always behave in the way realist theory prescribes for them: that leading states play the game of the balance of power, and potential victims of a would-be troublemaker ally themselves with the main defender of the status quo instead of joining the expansionist's bandwagon. The U.S. had certainly not behaved according to realist principles after World War I, and almost nobody followed Washington in the 1930s. One must therefore turn to more subjective factors. After all, ultimately the realist script is based on certain assumptions about how states behave in an anarchic milieu, but history shows that the nature of the milieu only encourages, not compels, them to behave according to these assumptions. What, then, made the United States decide to play this age-old game? The answer lies in the interaction of three factors.

The first, and probably the most important, was America's peculiar brand of nationalism as it had developed at the end of World War II. To call American nationalism ideological may sound like a pleonasm, since any nationalism can easily be analyzed as an ideology. But many nationalisms only assert the supremacy of the nation over other forms of social organization, or of one's own nation over others. What is special about what I call an ideological nationalism is its conviction that the greatness of the nation it favors lies in its standing for certain principles of universal validity. American nationalism at the end of the war was a blend of Wilsonianism and sense of power. The content of its ideology was the kind of liberal or Kantian philosophy of world affairs Woodrow Wilson had tried to promote abroad after he shifted from the isolationist version of American exceptionalism to the internationalist one.[2] Self-determination, self-government, free trade, international organization, and collective security for the solution of conflicts, a reasonably open diplomacy: these were Wilson's principles. But he had been singularly ambivalent about the role of power, especially coercive power, in international affairs; he preferred relying on the force of public opinion.[3] Such ambivalence did not plague the internationalism of the next generation of Wilsonians: Franklin D. Roosevelt and his successors. FDR tried to combine Wilsonian principles with a scheme for global management by the "Four Policemen" (two of whom were clients of the United States). When the United Nations Security Council, which was established by the war's winners, turned out to be paralyzed by Soviet vetoes, Roosevelt's successors put America, so to speak, in its place: as the secular arm of American ideals.

The American nationalism of the 1945–1949 period owes its potency to the combination of exceptional self-righteousness, derived from the conviction that the liberal principles on which the United States polity was based represent the best and highest ideal of social and world organization, with exceptional power and a determination to use it, especially given the absence of power elsewhere in the unstable or threatened parts of the world. The conviction of being not merely a "city on a hill" but a beacon for the world, allied to an untroubled capability, carried postwar America to impressive successes and some spectacular disasters.

What turned this enormous force in the direction of containment was a second factor. If the period of 1946–1949 is the formative experience of the whole postwar policy, the formative, traumatic experience that explains the course selected in 1946–1949 was the apparent failure of Roosevelt's Soviet policy. Before 1941, Soviet-American relations had been distant and rather cool, partly because of American anti-Communism, partly because of isolationism. After June 1941, earlier doubts became submerged in enthusiasm for the grant alliance, for the heroic resistance of the Soviet people and armies, and in hopes for postwar cooperation. John L. Gaddis, among others, had vigorously defended FDR from charges of naiveté in dealing with Stalin.[4] It is clear that Roosevelt's priority, rightly, was victory—which was unachievable without massive Soviet participation. It is also clear that he counted on a mix of American assets (such as economic resources and the bomb) as well as on the attractiveness for the Soviet Union of being recognized as a co-manager of world affairs, to channel Stalin's ambitions (beyond the security sphere FDR was prepared to grant to Moscow) in a cooperative direction. If this was not naive it did prove to be mistaken. FDR miscalculated Stalin's preferences and priorities. "Uncle Joe" was unwilling to let himself be trapped in schemes in which he would appear as a junior partner of the leading capitalist nation. He preferred to be the absolute master of his own domain and in a position to thwart the designs of American leaders. It wasn't, as Gaddis has written, that Stalin chose to make Soviet short-term interests and gains prevail over long-term ones; he simply had a very different and contentious reading of the Soviet Union's long-term interest. But the bitter experience of Soviet behavior in Poland, Iran, Turkey, at peace conferences, and in the U.N. was a shock, a lesson in disillusionment, from which American policymakers never fully recovered.

The collapse of plans and expectations that had mushroomed in the war years was not the same thing as a new policy. What shaped this was the third factor: the American "reading" of the Soviet Union that developed in 1946–1947 and about which so much has been written. Its most articulate expression remains George Kennan's "long telegram" and his article in *Foreign Affairs* of the spring of 1947. Soviet behavior was explained in terms of (surprise!) a blend of ideology and power: "no one should underrate the importance of dogma in Soviet affairs," and "everything must be done to advance the relative strength of the USSR as a factor of international society";[5] moreover, this behavior was presented as a necessity for the Soviet system, a formidable totalitarian machine that could not function without an external enemy. This interpretation had the merit of explaining why the Rooseveltian policy of cooperation had been bound to fail, as well as of suggesting the kind of policy that could succeed: containment. Barriers, not bargains, were the only things that would work. It also had the merit of legitimizing the continuing promotion and export of the Wilsonian ideals across the non-Communist world, and the application of American power on their behalf.

America's ideology made impossible the acceptance of a Soviet sphere, not merely of interest but of domination, in Eastern Europe. America's reading of the Soviet blend of ideology and power made it impossible for Americans to believe that the Soviet Union would be satisfied with only such a sphere anyhow; for it was seen as a revolutionary force determined to push for violent revolution everywhere. And the Wilsonian ideology endorses only those revolutions that quickly lead to democratic processes and institutions (few do so!).

The three elements I have described combined to give U.S. policy toward the Soviet Union its propulsive force over many years. The United States of 1947–1948 was ready for Kennan and Hans Morgenthau: for the grafting of "power politics" onto the Wilsonian worldview (as Michael Hunt puts it,[6] there was a common foe: isolationism)—or rather, to change the metaphor, for placing the motor of realism into the body of the Wilsonian car. The U.S. was ready for a reading of Soviet behavior that explained past frustrations, present challenges, and the proper course for the future. The same blend of ingredients also explains why the course was to be containment, not a "shoot-out at High Noon:" Soviet "mellowing," not unconditional surrender, was the ultimate aim. Wilsonianism had demonstrated twice, in 1917 and 1941, that America, when provoked, could wage war until total victory; but the liberal ideology is squeamish about initiating wars and prefers that the sinners reform (if they are willing) rather than their having to be destroyed. Kennan's reading of the Soviets stated both that they were impermeable to blandishments or exhortations, *and* that they were susceptible to changing their behavior if blocked with constancy and determination. For those reasons, and also, of course, thanks to America's vast power, there was no inevitable Armageddon, only the need to remain strong and to deprive the rival of any hope of winning either by surprise or piece by piece.

But the blend had its flaws. Three had to do with the interpretation of the enemy's behavior. First, insofar as the canonical version put a heavy emphasis on the importance of Communist ideology, did this mean that the enemy was communism and not merely the Soviet Union? Or was it Soviet might and hostility, rather than Marxism-Leninism, that made Moscow dangerous? Gaddis has shown[7] that both the Truman and the Eisenhower administrations never gave up the hope of splitting the "Communist bloc," either through incentives (Truman) or through pressure (Eisenhower); but the United States has been far better at exploiting than at provoking splits precisely because of a tendency to see communism as inherently evil—unless and until a Communist regime turns against Moscow.

Second, the same emphasis on Communist ideology and the view of the U.S.S.R as a relentless, driven challenger of the status quo have combined to produce a frequently oversimplified reading of world politics—a frenzied and overheated one in which Americans take far too seriously Soviet rhetoric about world revolution, or the class struggle, or the fall of capitalism, and above all tend to interpret discrete events and disparate troubles as if they were all parts of a Soviet master plan: the familiar triumph of a crude "globalism" over the more sober analyses of local realities. (The Soviets, in a "mirror image" of the United States, also tend to take American rhetoric at face value and see plots and grand designs where there are often only improvisations and tactical moves.)

Third, while Kennan's interpretation of Soviet behavior ruled out one explanation of Soviet conduct—the "defensive" view, which sees the U.S.S.R. as a power concerned above all with its own security (a view to which Kennan himself came close later on), it left room for a variety of subinterpretations, so to speak. Alexander Dallin and Gail Lapidus have distinguished "essentialists" who focus not on what Moscow does but on what it is, "mechanists" concerned with Soviet behavior, and "interactionists" interested in differences within the Soviet elite and in the effects of American behavior on Soviet policy;[8] one can also separate those who believe in planned and constant expansion from those who see the Soviet Union as more of an exploiter of opportunities.[9] Needless to say, each version has different implications for U.S. behavior.

Two other flaws affect American policy directly. One concerns the ultimate objective of containment. Is it to change Soviet external behavior to one that would make Soviet leaders more committed to the status quo and concerned with moderation and "stability?" This has been the official intention of most American administrations; but insofar as—Kennan *dixit*—Soviet conduct abroad is determined by the nature of the Soviet system, how could external behavior be lastingly transformed without a change in the nature of the regime? Could, for instance, the Soviet empire in Eastern Europe change its nature— turning into a mere sphere of interest—without a profound transformation of the Soviet regime? And if this is indeed the case, shouldn't that transformation become a goal of U.S. policy? And if so, could it be best accomplished through pressure and confrontation, or through cooperation? The original consensus left great leeway for disputes on these questions, and also on the question of whether it was at all realistic to expect a change in external behavior that would amount to Soviet acceptance of the American, or Western, code of conduct.

The original consensus also left room for another uncertainty. The world only partly, or fitfully, matched the vision of a contest between democracies and communism. Many countries were autocracies; others had been colonized, were struggling against foreign rule, and risked turning to Moscow for support. How should the United States deal with these "gray" cases? Should it give priority to anticommunism (or anti-Sovietism) in the name of power realities but at the cost of sullying democratic ideals? Or should it insist on democratic reform and support nationalist anti- or postcolonial forces in the name of self-determination or self-government, even if communism (or Moscow) might be the ultimate beneficiary? American leaders have had trouble being consistent. Eisenhower's anticommunist priority in the Middle East, which led him to confront Nasser by canceling aid for the Aswan Dam and by sending Marines to Lebanon, nevertheless made him rescue Nasser from the British, the French and the Israelis at Suez, so that Third World nationalism would not fall into the arms of the Soviets. President Kennedy wanted to champion diversity and to encourage nationalism, yet he sometimes blamed the Soviets for breeding revolutionary movements everywhere.

There are two other notable legacies of the formative period. One, at least, deserves far more scrutiny than can be provided here. The United States of 1946–1949 manifested both a considerable hubris of power (much of it, initially, centered on the possession of the bomb, much of it derived from the experience of successful alliance management in World War II) and a remarkable insecurity, which translated itself not only into McCarthyism at home but also into exaggerations of both Soviet power and its evil designs. As I have already argued, the official interpretation of Moscow's policy explains the tendency (still displayed by Jimmy Carter after the Soviet invasion of Afghanistan) to read too much into Soviet moves, or to read Soviet machinations into Communist or leftist revolutionary acts outside the realm controlled by Moscow; but it does not account for the exaggerations of Soviet power (as shown, for instance, in NSC 68). There was going to be a long history, not only of self-deterrence in the years when the U.S. enjoyed a nuclear monopoly (a self-restraint reasonably easy to explain rationally) but also of self-scares: bomber gaps, Sputnik terror, missile gaps, nightmare scenarios of "windows of vulnerability," false beliefs about the size and degree of readiness of Soviet conventional armies. These tell us a great deal about either the tendency to see an enemy so different as to be ten feet tall, or the fears of inadequacy (a legacy of Pearl Harbor, perhaps?) lurking behind the self-confidence and capability. They remind us, if we need to be so reminded, that next to a history written in terms of power realities and long-range trends, there is also a history of perceptions, misperceptions, and short-range, wild fluctuations in the assessment of the adversary.

The second legacy may be easier to explain. I would call it the bipolar obsession: the tendency to look at the world as if the contest between Washington and Moscow explained almost everything that occurs in it, as if the military dimension of power remained as decisive as in the past, and so therefore those actors who weigh far less than the "Big Two" on the scales of military power would deserve far less attention. To be sure, academics since the early 1970s have written abundantly about the "rise of the trading state," or about the areas of "complex interdependence" in which force plays only a distant role; indeed, this academic (if I may borrow Ollie North's contagious way of replacing "I" with "this lieutenant-colonel") has stressed since the mid-1960s the relative impotence of military giants in the nuclear age. And yet there is a continuing disconnection between the manifest complexities of power and power hierarchies in the present world, and the obsessive focus on Soviet-American relations. For the Soviet Union, the United States cannot but appear as the archrival—the wall it finds at the end of every walk or excursion. But for the United States, which so often proclaims the limitations of Soviet power—pointing out that the only strong Soviet suit is a uniform—the reason for official preoccupation with the Soviet-American relationship is not so self-evident. To be sure, global peace is at stake. But there are deeper reasons: for the United States, this is a way of perpetuating, somehow, a world that is no more—the world of 1945–1949, in which only two powers seemed to matter. American behavior in world affairs displays uneasiness with complexity; there is a quest for certainty and predictability that affects both American foreign policy and the American approach to the discipline of international relations. A multipolar world, or a world in which the different components of power are somehow disconnected, is hard to grasp and harder even to manage. Bipolarity, which focuses on the dimension of power that is still America's strongest, provides a sort of nostalgic reassurance.

Relations

Rather than producing a sketchy history of the Cold War, I will list some of the features that strike me as the most important or intriguing after more than forty years of contentious relations.

Like all the other contests among rivals competing for hegemony in world affairs, the Cold War has been a battle for power and influence, especially over the areas around the borders of the Soviet Union; but the many ways in which power can be applied far from one's borders, and in particular the importance of military and economic assistance, have given a worldwide scope to the struggle, especially after Stalin's death. This global scope has, of course, been largely fostered by the second aspect of the contest: its ideological one. The Soviets have supported not only communist movements challenging the United States and its allies, but other forces of national liberation or social revolution as well, and the United States has resorted both to political and to military means to encourage and support anti-Soviet "freedom fighters," not only in the areas into which the Soviets were trying to expand but also in some of those they control. Not every power contest in history has had this ideological dimension, at least in peacetime.

However, unlike comparable rivalries, this one has not led to a shooting war between the adversaries—a fact that now appears overdetermined, but was by no means assured or deemed likely by all American policymakers. Kenneth Waltz's argument that bipolar systems are inherently more stable than multipolar ones[10] I continue to find profoundly unconvincing, for all the reasons he gives might just as well lead to armed conflict (indeed, bipolar contests usually degenerate into wars because of the very delicacy of the balance: marginal shifts— the defection of an ally, the alignment of a former neutral power—risk destroying it). I would put much more emphasis on other factors. One is the determination of *these* two rivals to avoid another conflagration so soon after the end of World War II, a determination buttressed in Moscow's case by an ideology that promises ultimate Communist victory through the inevitable march of progressive social forces, and in Washington's case by the combination of Wilsonianism and interpretation of Soviet behavior mentioned before. Another factor is the relative independence of the two rivals from each other: no common, contested border, and very little trade. To be sure, the armies of the two blocs have confronted each other along a common border, but that border is in Germany. A vacuum of power could still have led to violent conflict, with one side expanding and the other one resisting; this happened in Korea, although not between the U.S. and the Soviet Union. But there is a third factor: nuclear deterrence. It did not become fully mutual until the late 1950s; but in the earlier period, there was considerable American reluctance to use nuclear weapons partly because ultimate "victory" at low cost seemed possible, albeit later, partly because of the opposition of allies who were exposed to Soviet invasion.[11] As a result, there were attempts at nuclear blackmail, but they were rare, obliquely aimed at the Soviet Union, and made with considerable ambivalence.[12] And war was replaced by crises, each one of which was geographically as well as politically contained.

The contest has continued nevertheless. As many of the critics of containment have pointed out, the building of situations of strength has led sometimes to tests of strength (and will), sometimes to truces, but not to the grand accommodation that defenders of the policy had, at times, promised. However, those critics who thirst for a more aggressive, or less "reactive," policy have never prevailed precisely because they appeared dangerously addicted to high risks: survival may not be enough, but it's a prerequisite. And those critics who pleaded for accommodation soon had not only the memory of Munich and above all of FDR's disappointment to contend with, they could also never quite cope with the ideological dimension of the struggle. Power conflicts and clashes of interests are said to be easier to steer toward compromises (not always!). But even though the ideological component may be less visible and prominent now than in the late 1940s—on the Soviet side because of the new pragmatism, for the United States because of an increasing contradiction between the view of the Soviet Union as an evil empire and the search for agreements—it remains important enough to prevent the giant settlement some have dreamed about and to make political cooperation, for instance over regional conflicts, very difficult. The Soviets can, in practice, behave with prudence and even retrench. They can even try to join the international economic agencies of capitalism. But they cannot abandon their faith in the ultimate superiority of socialism over the free enterprise system, or their "progressive" reading of history. In other words, they may deem the Western system of international order usable and even advantageous for some of their purposes, but they cannot proclaim it legitimate. (Moreover, in terms of sheer power, they cannot easily drop or sell out their friends, nor often compel them to accept deals cooked up with the United States.)

The same is true on the American side. The United States government has dealt with the Soviet government as a legitimate one, insofar as Washington has never tried to undermine it at home (even if some members of the Reagan administration have muttered about the impossibility of signing agreements with a totalitarian regime); a wish for a different system is not the same thing as a policy. However, Washington has never considered Soviet external behavior, or the Soviet empire in Eastern Europe, to be legitimate. Nor has the United States heeded Soviet demands to be treated as an equal superpower, not only on paper but also in deeds. And as long as such American attitudes persist, Moscow sees *its* legitimacy threatened. This has been the story so far. The Cold War is a relationship that developed between two limits: no direct military conflict, no condominium or grand, final settlement.

Within these limits, each U.S. administration has had its own profile and its own surprises or paradoxes. The Truman administration, having proclaimed a universal doctrine, got bogged down applying it in the one area in which it had been most reluctant to get stuck—Southeast Asia. The Eisenhower administration came in with the rhetoric of rollback and the strategy of massive retaliation, but it liquidated one war (Korea), stayed out of another one (Indochina), did not let itself be stampeded by Krushchev's ballistic missiles bluff, and began a dialogue with Moscow. John F. Kennedy started with a trumpet call, but after the Cuban missile crisis moved in a direction that suggested that nuclear weapons were more dangerous than communism. Lyndon Johnson sacrificed broader foreign policy goals to Vietnam, but he too tried to pursue arms control at the very end. Nixon's course has been studied ad nauseam: a limited détente, largely prompted by the desire to get Moscow's help for extrication from Vietnam, soon became a more ambitious, triangular strategy involving China, but one that was beginning to run into serious trouble by the time the president resigned. Gerald Ford in just about two years saw much of Henry Kissinger's policy disintegrate, and even dropped the word détente. Jimmy Carter began by proclaiming the end of the bipolar obsession and the advent of a new agenda. He continued by pursuing simultaneously two incompatible policies—one pragmatic and accommodating, the other one confrontational—and he ended by emphasizing the second after the Soviet invasion of Afghanistan. Ronald Reagan's beginning was probably the most combative ever, but after 1984 the direction was one that his earliest supporters viewed with consternation.

What lesson can one derive from this potted outline? Discontinuity between each administration and the next? On the surface, yes, but the variations are superficial; or rather, they are greater within each administration's time span than among administrations. Truman, Eisenhower, and Kennedy showed remarkable steadfastness over Berlin. As shown by Gaddis[13] (whom I keep quoting, because he is the ablest historian of the period), Eisenhower's "New Look" had its antecedents in the Truman period, just as JFK's test ban had its own in Ike's time. SALT II came out looking very much like the 1974 Vladivostok deal that Carter had at first disdained, and Reagan's rearmament merely continued what the late Carter administration had begun.

Another lesson points to a different sort of discontinuity: it is the difficulty of arriving at a steady relationship. The domestic reasons for this will be examined below, and my previous discussion of accommodation and legitimacy is also part of the explanation. Another one is that Soviet and American leaders have rarely been on the same wavelength: Eisenhower, for all his moderation, was too suspicious and Krushchev was too contradictory and truculent; Carter had to deal with an ossified Brezhnev; in 1986–1987, Gorbachev talked a bit like the early Carter, but he faced Reagan (the partly "converted" Reagan of 1987–1988 was a lame duck).

The deepest reasons are these. First, it is of the very essence of "containment" that every Soviet attempt at expanding power or influence will either bring about an American response or, if it fails to do so, a storm in the United States. Therefore, the history of the relationship is bound to be a succession of minor or major shocks that could have been avoided only if the United States had become entirely passive or if the Soviet Union had been willing to pass up opportunities to stop seeking or supporting clients. Second, America's policy instruments are much better at containing than at forcing the Soviet Union into lasting self-containment and conciliation. Trade and credits never became a major source of rewards and punishment: when the United States has tried to use them for sanctions, the Soviet Union has always turned to America's allies. Diplomacy has been an important instrument, either directly, in areas of common interest (what might be called the substitute for a new European settlement—the complex of agreements on Berlin and at Helsinki—as well as arms control), or indirectly, when Kissinger played his China card—but the uses of the latter are limited both by the fact that any shift from a "friendly" U.S.–China relation to a quasi-alliance hardens the Soviets (as Brzezinski found out) and by China's own reluctance to mortgage its independence and diplomatic subtlety. Cultural relations and ties between private U.S. entrepreneurs and the Soviet Union have been limited by the nature of the Soviet system. Linkage briefly played a minor role, but the extent to which it led the Soviet Union to pressure North Vietnam into a compromise in 1972 remains debatable, and Kissinger, the chief architect of linkage, became increasingly concerned with safeguarding arms control. Indeed, there is more evidence of what might be called negative linkage—the weakening of arms control when the political climate worsens, as in 1968, 1975–1976, 1979–1983—than of positive linkage—the successful use of this technique to expand the areas of agreement on terms favorable to the West.

Lovers of paradox might come to the conclusion that America's favorite instrument of containment—military power, despite Kennan's reservations—may also have turned out to be the best tool for bringing about partial détente: arms control is the safety valve of a nuclear arms race in which most of the initiatives have been taken by the United States (Michael Mandelbaum has described the U. S. as the innovator and model for the U.S.S.R.)—a safety valve whose theory and main concepts were also developed in America.[14]

Indeed, for all its rockiness, the Soviet-American relationship has shown some lasting features, and the most striking is the growing importance of the nuclear component. Both sides appear to have tied themselves into nuclear Gordian knots. Both proclaim that nuclear wars can't be won and shouldn't be fought. Each one, for its own reasons, has developed a formidable war-fighting capacity, shifted from "existential deterrence" to deterrence based on the threat of waging nuclear war, and thus undermined both crisis and arms race stability. Both sides rely, for deterrence, on weapons that threaten thousands of targets—the targets having multiplied to justify the capabilities—yet a "rational" use of these weapons would prove impossible in an armed conflict, and they might be very hard to control in an acute crisis.[15] Both sides, as a result, have been driven into attempting to square the circle: to safeguard nuclear deterrence, for it has preserved peace better than conventional deterrence in the past, while reducing the risks of actual nuclear use. Joseph S. Nye, Jr., has ably shown how much "nuclear learning" has taken place, and what (limited) nuclear regimes have developed.[16] With each side determined to maintain an invulnerable second strike force, not only the quest for superiority but also the endless addition of new war-fighting capabilities seem wasteful and absurd as well as dangerous. The logic of nuclear weaponry has led the superpowers both to constant expansions of their arsenals and to a recurrent search for regulation. Every administration since Eisenhower's has been engaged in this quest, even when its relations with Moscow had at first been tense or icy, even when its predecessor's attempt at arms control had failed.

This search is part of another major feature: the emergence of "rules of the game," developed informally more than through treaties (with the exception of Helsinki and the arms control treaties), by trial and error even more than by agreement. I have examined in detail these rules elsewhere, with their limits and ambiguities.[17] While each side has on the whole respected the other's sphere of vital interests and been prudent about exploiting defections, this has not prevented avid competition in gray areas and the application of the Reagan doctrine. But not even the return to the Cold War of 1980–1983 meant the demise of the rules—Reagan observed provisions of SALT II although he had termed them "fatally flawed," and the launching of the Strategic Defense Initiative did not lead to the abrogation of the ABM treaty. Indeed, the development of these rules and the very fear of falling into unmanageable crises have resulted in one striking fact: since 1962, there has been no drama like the Cuban missile crisis.

Still another feature is the overextension of both rivals, although for different reasons. In the Soviet case, the main cause is the one so openly admitted by the current "new thinking:" the inefficiency of the Soviet economic system, except in the production of largely unusable weapons. In the American case, there is also a considerable gap between resources and commitments, which recent studies by Robert Gilpin and Paul Kennedy have brought to light; but this is mainly because of the gigantic scope of America's postwar commitments. As some critics have pointed out, containment—the attempt to keep the Soviet Union within the spheres it had come to occupy by the end of World War II—resulted, contrary to Kennan's hopes, not in a multipolar world but in an American policy that regarded the whole non-Communist world as America's sphere of influence, a sphere in which threatening developments had to be resisted.[19] This, indeed, is one of the reasons that a condominium has been so firmly ruled out, as well as any lesser formula that might appear to recognize a Soviet right to participate in shaping the fate of these regions, and one of the reasons that the détente of the 1970s collapsed: the United States saw Soviet "geopolitical expansion" as intolerable, while Moscow deemed America's policies in the Middle East, Africa, and Asia malevolent and domineering and hoped that Washington would resign itself to a less favorable "correlation of forces."[20] In multiple forms—military bases and assistance, economic aid to friendly regimes, the cooperation of secret services, covert operations, the resort to proxies, subsidies to political clients in other countries—containment of the Soviet Union has led to a more or less subtle American hegemony. But the resources of some of the clients and allies have grown much faster than America's, and the expenditures of the U.S. government have risen faster than the American GNP. The success of the American way of containment carries within it the seeds of America's (relative) decline.

Domestic Politics

In no country is foreign policy less isolated from domestic politics and pressures than in the United States. To what extent have American attitudes and policies toward the Soviet Union been shaped by them? We need to distinguish three different levels.

The first is public opinion—the beliefs of the general public. They appear to have been reasonably constant. The public has had, throughout the years of containment, two main concerns: that there be no war (a war it has often deemed far more likely than have the elites) and that the United States not be weak. On the whole, it has been supportive of official policy, merely pulling toward the pole of strength whenever it became concerned, less perhaps about Soviet "superiority" than about a deterioration of America's position in the world (as in the second half of the 1970s), and toward the pole of peace whenever it felt that policy was becoming too confrontational (as in the early 1980s). Distrust of the Soviet Union is deep—a result of a vast amount of ignorance (Soviet visitors are shocked by the American tendency to minimize the huge Soviet contribution to victory over Hitler) and of considerable dislike for much of what is known about Soviet society and politics. The idea of extensive political cooperation with Moscow has never been the public's preferred scenario. Nevertheless, the latest study by the Chicago Council on Foreign Relations[21] shows that the general public favors arms control agreements, cultural and scientific exchanges, grain sales, and unrestricted trade. It is willing to defend Western Europe against a Soviet attack and ambivalent about the first use of nuclear weapons by the United States: hostile in principle, but less so if the result of not using them would give a strategic advantage to the Soviets. The idea of SDI is popular, but this seems to be primarily an expression of the unease caused by the offensive nuclear weapons race. Basically, the public seems to see no other ways to alleviate this unease than arms control (which the threat of SDI might facilitate) and an improved political climate in U.S.–Soviet relations.

None of this can be seen as a serious restraint on a foreign policy that aims at avoiding both war and condominium. Indeed, it may well reflect official policy rather than inspire it. At times, American leaders may have misjudged the public's willingness to support their policies. Gaddis blames FDR for having exaggerated the scope of isolationism in 1944–1945 and failing to "prepare the American people for the kind of realistic settlement his own instincts told him would be inevitable."[22] Ernest May believes that in the early years of the Cold War the administration first understated and then overstated the Soviet menace in order to keep abreast of the public.[23] Be that as it may, the only two warning lights that need to be taken seriously by policymakers seem to be, first, the permanent need not to pursue either too "hard" or too "soft" a line (neither 1914 nor 1939!) and the recent evidence of considerable skepticism toward official U.S. foreign policy in the generation under forty-five. More important, perhaps, is the fact that today the crucial foreign policy issue is defined by the public (and the leaders as well) as the arms race rather than relations with the Soviet Union.

The second level is that of the leaders or elites—a category that includes the politicians and other Americans in senior positions with knowledge of international affairs. They are more "internationalist" (and willing to intervene militarily abroad) than the public, and also more "threat-conscious." But the main feature here is the increasing polarization of the political elites since the end of the 1960s, not so much on the Soviet Union itself (almost all, we are told, are both suspicious of Moscow and favorable to arms control) as on issues that affect containment policies deeply: American actions in the Third World and military spending. This means that an administration may have difficulty in obtaining a consensus among the elites on whatever course of action is devised, either because the course is deemed too tough or too soft by some or because it is too balanced or complex to obtain strong support on either side of the divide. The second case is that of the Kissinger détente policy, which ran into a coalition of liberals critical of its apparent amorality (on human rights in the Soviet Union as well as because of its interventionism, inspired by anti-Soviet considerations, in places like Chile, or on Pakistan's side during the Bangladesh war), and conservatives worried about the military balance and distrustful of agreements with the Soviets. The consensus of the old foreign policy "Establishment" on containment never recovered from the shock of Vietnam; détente was conceived largely outside the consensus, and did not mobilize it in the old way. The split in the Carter administration reflected its new division, and its influence has constantly diminished anyhow.

The most important level, therefore, is the third: organized political forces, which include both the various movements and pressure groups concerned with foreign policy, and America's political institutions. We are dealing here both with the elites harnessed for specific action and with the portion of the public they succeed in mobilizing. This is the level about which officials have to be most concerned. There are four issues that tend to cause trouble. The first is a kind of built-in imbalance in the U.S. polity: it leans to the right. The reasons for this tilt are numerous: the development, since World War II, of a complex national security bureaucracy that includes the military services, extends to the contractors who work for it, and attracts those that benefit from it; the lack of sympathy or understanding for the forces of radical change in the developing countries; the hold of what might be called Cold War realism, whose emergence I have discussed above; the power of conservative views in both parties; the American labor movement's own anticommunism in the postwar era; the fact that many of those who do not favor vast military buildups or extensive interventions abroad whether through force or through military assistance are residual isolationists with little effect on the major parties and on foreign policy debates.

I do not mean to say that there is no constituency for "leftist" causes: the rise of the nuclear freeze movement in the early 1980s was spectacular. But its staying power was weak; it was more a reaction to a sudden fear of confrontation than a disciplined and coherent lobby. This doesn't mean that it had no effect—the move Ronald Reagan made in 1984 toward a new dialogue with Moscow was probably a reaction to it; but it certainly did not impose its agenda on the American political process. Compare the effectiveness of the Committee on the Present Danger in the period of 1976–1979 with that of the antinuclear movement: the second comprised political amateurs in comparison with the first.[24] Pressure from the right forced a weak President Ford to move away from an arms control agreement in 1976 and to drop any mention of détente. It was, I would argue, fear of the right that led Nixon, and to some extent Kissinger (who, William Hyland tells us, had no illusion about a deep transformation of U.S.–Soviet relations),[25] to "oversell" détente, presenting it as a successful way of modifying Soviet behavior—a strategy that backfired badly. The armed forces and their supporters, who are prone to endorse arms control only as long as new weapons systems are launched to compensate for them, are certainly more influential than the advocates of reduced deterrence.

The other three issues concern the peculiar American institutional system. One is the major role played by Congress under the Constitution (a role so important that administrations have been trying to find ways of circumventing the legislative branch, ranging from executive agreements to the elevation of the National Security Adviser and to President Reagan's Iran-contra "junta"). On the one hand, it is the need to obtain congressional support that has often led presidents to exaggerate the intensity and scope of the Soviet threat: from Dean Acheson's famous defense of aid to Greece through the image of one rotten apple (a Communist Greece) infecting the whole barrel (the rest of Europe) and Truman's decision to present a universal doctrine rather than a mere program to aid Greece and Turkey, to LBJ justifying American military intervention in Vietnam in terms of the domino theory, to Caspar Weinberger trying to "sell" SDI as a response to an ominous Soviet program of defenses, or Reagan resorting to scary hyperbole about Central America or the Persian Gulf. On the other hand, Congress has a way of making the execution of foreign policy more difficult, at least since 1972, when the twenty-year period of congressional deference to the executive branch ended. The Jackson amendment to the SALT I treaty, ordering negotiators to aim at equal numbers of weapons in future talks, and above all the Jackson-Vanik amendment and the decision of the Senate to cut off assistance to "friendly" forces in Angola, are usually cited as examples of the way in which Congress removed both carrots and sticks from a policy that had relied on both. Indeed, congressional interference makes a complex policy of linkage very difficult, insofar as such a policy requires full control of the policy instruments by the executive. The Senate's growing suspicion of the Soviet Union, fueled both by Soviet actions and by the Committee on the Present Danger, complicated Carter's already bungled attempts to conclude a SALT II treaty and to get it ratified. The debate on ratification of the INF treaty by the Senate shows that the executive's predicament in Congress remains unenviable.

The next institutional issue is the presidential system itself. Each administration, especially if it has a different political color from the one that preceded it, feels a need to appear to start from scratch and to react against its predecessor's mistakes. Changes in the strategy of containment have at least as often resulted from such domestic shifts as from changes in Soviet behavior. And so we have had rollback offered as an improvement on containment in the early 1950s to please Republicans; the missile gap of 1960 that turned out not to exist; and we had Carter's sudden new arms control proposal of March 1977. The impression of discontinuity is greater than the reality, but this impression contributes to the inherent turbulence of U.S.–Soviet relations. The fact that the leading figures of each administration in foreign policy are political appointees, not career diplomats, and that the nonpartisan personalities who served Democratic as well as Republican presidents in the 1940s, 1950s, and 1960s have almost disappeared, heightens the sense of "stop and go," if not discontinuity.

The last institutional factor is the fragmentation of the executive itself. Often, in negotiations with the Soviets, the rivalry between the NSC and the State Department has wrecked policy.[26] Inevitably, the NSC staff and adviser—located in the White House—have their eyes not only on national security but on the domestic political effects of particular policies on the president. This makes not only for intragovernmental conflict but for Soviet-American tension whenever the domestic political climate seems to require that the president appease or mend fences with forces on the right. Moreover, as is well known, the NSC has no institutional memory.

All these issues complicate Soviet-American relations, not only on the American side, by politicizing the process of policymaking and limiting the President's freedom of action, but also on the Soviet side, by creating distrust because of the difficulty the Soviets have in understanding the complexities of the U.S. political system. The Soviets tend both to attribute excessive significance to every statement made by a legislator or a member of the executive and to impute to the president far more power and far more leeway than he has, perhaps because so much of their own experience derives not only from their own regime but also from their contacts with political systems in which the executive enjoys considerable freedom of maneuver and decision.

The Alliance

The Western Alliance remains the most successful achievement of the containment policy. Western Europe has been neither conquered nor "Finlandized." Its postwar recovery and economic growth have been spectacular. The European Economic Community—an entity whose creation and development the United States has supported—is progressing, albeit slowly. NATO, as a military institution, has survived repeated crises and gloomy predictions. It has served remarkably well the essential interests of both the U.S. and its major allies. And yet, like all good things, the Alliance is also a source of complications in U.S.–Soviet relations.

Let us look at the past forty years. The Alliance has been, for the United States:

1. *A source of ambivalence.* Gaddis has documented the early Bohlen-Kennan debate concerning U.S. policy toward Western Europe:[27] should it aim at creating an independent center of power, given America's limited resources and perhaps wisdom—or a sphere of dependents, given the Europeans' own fragmentation and their security need for a U.S. military presence and nuclear guarantee? Initially, both the British and the West Germans preferred the latter. U.S. policy has consisted of, on the one hand, supporting Western European integration, but on the other trying to make sure that the new entity adopts economic policies that wouldn't harm America's interests, and above all preventing it from spilling over into the domain of foreign policy and defense, which are the preserve of NATO—

under American domination. As a result, the United States has, on the whole, remained the principal provider of weapons for NATO as well as the main interlocutor of the Soviet Union, capable of speaking for itself and for NATO; but this situation has often led Washington to complain that the West Europeans rely too much on America in the realm of security and do not contribute enough to the common defense.

2. *A focal point of tension.* This condition was inevitable. Western Europe was seen as the main stake of the Soviet-American contest. The early negotiations on the future of Germany and the successive Berlin crises were among the high points of the Cold War. Soviet or Soviet-sponsored initiatives to repress rebellions in Eastern Europe have always raised the temperature in the Western part of the continent. However, the West Europeans themselves have tried to remove themselves as much as possible from the conflict. The détente policy launched in 1964 by de Gaulle and followed by the West Germans worried American leaders at first, but the final result—at Helsinki—has effectively both confirmed the division of Europe that was one of the main results of World War II and substituted a process of bargaining and exchanges for the earlier threats and crises.

3. *A goal.* Indeed, it was the Allies' itch for détente that prodded Nixon and Kissinger in 1969–1970. They did not want Moscow to obtain from the West Europeans benefits that Washington itself wished to provide to the Soviets in exchange for agreements far exceeding the scope of those that most interested the Allies (Berlin and some security measures in Europe). Similarly, the resumption of arms control proposals by the Reagan administration at the end of 1981, despite its initial hostility, was a result of West European anxieties about the collapse of the U.S.–Soviet détente. Reagan's further shift of 1984–1985 was also partly a response to these fears.

4. *A brake.* At times, it was the Allies who worried that the United States and the Soviets were getting a bit too close, at the possible expense of the European interests. In 1960–1962, the two old men of Europe—de Gaulle and Adenauer—adopted a much harder line on Berlin than the Eisenhower and especially the Kennedy administrations. After the Reykjavik summit meeting of 1986, Allied complaints about Reagan's sudden enthusiastic participation in the undermining of nuclear deterrence (already manifest in SDI) obliged the administration to retreat from its apparent endorsement of the goal of abolishing all ballistic nuclear missiles. At other times, the Allies have acted as a

brake on American impulses for confrontation. Their reluctance to impose sanctions on the Soviets after Afghanistan and their refusal to ban agreements with Moscow on the gas pipeline and advanced technology slowed American efforts in the first case and thwarted them in the second.

5. *A cause for worry*. American officials have been disturbed each time a West European leader embarked on a foreign policy that appeared to diverge from America's own course toward the U.S.S.R. De Gaulle's nuclear policy, and his attempt at giving to the EEC a foreign affairs and defense dimension in 1961–1962, followed by his offer of "détente, entente, and cooperation" to Moscow antagonized Washington. Brandt's *Ostpolitik* deeply disturbed American leaders at first. Washington is also disturbed by the evolution of West German opinion, and part of the Federal Republic's political class, on the nuclear issue since the early 1980s—a subject that led to a Franco-American rapprochement in that period. Nor did American officialdom approve of the separate line taken by the West Europeans in 1973–1981 on the Arab-Israeli conflict, which they refused to treat as a subset of the U.S.–Soviet contest.

If we move from the past to the present, we find that the nuclear component of the Soviet-American relationship has also become the main bone of contention in the U.S.–West European one (to the extent—limited—that one can talk of *a* West European position). The United States and its Allies have very different attitudes, which reflect to a large extent an immutable reality: geography. The deterrence of any Soviet attack on Western Europe is the main reason that the United States has always refused to commit itself to a no-first-use position on nuclear weapons. Indeed, the need to have on European soil nuclear weapon systems capable of hitting military targets not only in Eastern Europe but also in the Soviet Union was the main reason for the missile deployments of 1983–1987. Soviet proposals for many years have aimed not at a dissolution of NATO or even at a withdrawal of U.S. ground forces, which would risk leaving West Germany as the preponderant military (as well as economic) power on the Western side of Europe and might "delegitimize" Soviet military and political domination in Eastern Europe. Instead, their goal has been the denuclearization of European NATO, so as both to force the Alliance to rely primarily on conventional deterrence—a difficult enterprise, given the Warsaw Pact's advantages—and to remove a number of American war-fighting weapon systems threatening to the Soviets.

Nuclear deterrence consisting of a threat of a first use has served to offset the Soviet conventional advantage; and despite the all-too-logical arguments of those who complain that such a threat is not credible in an era in which the superpowers' nuclear arsenals are roughly equal, uncertainty about the American reaction to a Soviet conventional thrust—the fact that the Soviets can't be sure the threat is a bluff—has kept deterrence from failing. But Americans in recent years have become increasingly dubious about a nuclear war-fighting strategy should nuclear deterrence fail and worried about the wisdom of relying for deterrence on "threats of escalation that would ensure (NATO's) own destruction."[28] Indeed, nuclear war rather than the Soviet Union has gradually become the chief danger. However, many West Europeans remain deeply troubled by conventional deterrence, and confident in the solidity of nuclear deterrence, if it is provided, so to speak, at every rung of the escalation ladder. And many of those mainstream West Europeans who are as fearful of nuclear war and as uncertain that nuclear deterrence is foolproof as the Americans nevertheless diverge even more from American positions, insofar as they want either the end of NATO, or a drastic "alternative" defense system, or at least a denuclearized central front.

Thus we face a paradoxical situation. Almost all the West Europeans want to preserve the benefits of the Soviet-European détente of the early 1970s and subscribe to the goals recently described by Helmut Kohl and Erich Honecker during the East German leader's visit to the Federal Republic (even though some Frenchmen suspect the West Germans of really aiming at reunification): a reduction of tensions and the erosion (but not the removal) of the barriers that divide Europe. In this respect, West Europeans are far ahead of the cool American-Soviet relationship. But in the nuclear realm, the Americans increasingly tend to separate deterrence from nuclear use. Nuclear deterrence is still their policy, but, on the one hand, they now want to try to deemphasize it. "Decreasing reliance on nuclear weapons" has become a slogan, shared by the U.S. Catholic Bishops and strategists at Harvard's Kennedy School of Government. On the other hand, Americans believe deterrence can be maintained even without the missiles deployed in 1983–1987, as long as the United States makes clear that it stands by its commitment and preserves a variety of other systems—including tactical nuclear armaments on the continent—capable of hitting Soviet military targets. However, they make no secret of their conviction that any actual resort to nuclear weapons in Europe would be hard to control and probably disastrous. Here, the mainstream West Europeans lag far behind the "new thinking" of the United States.

West Europeans believe that a proclaimed reluctance to use nuclear weapons first undermines nuclear deterrence, *and* that the credibility of deterrence requires an extensive capability, based in Western Europe itself, for fighting a nuclear war on Soviet soil. Today, in this triangular relationship, there is a West European–Soviet political and economic connection stronger than the Soviet-American one, and a new U.S.–Soviet nuclear convergence (concerning, so far, only the European battlefield) that deeply worries many West Europeans, for three reasons at least: because it seems to destroy, through U.S.–Soviet collusion, the consensus on a NATO strategy painfully arrived at in the 1960s; because it threatens to magnify divisions among the West Europeans—splitting off the West Germans, most of whom, for obvious reasons, see nuclear weapons on the continent as threats to their own survival, or as provocative rather than as an assurance of peace; and because it will sooner or later make it difficult for the British and the French to keep their expanding nuclear forces out of the negotiations.

Prospects

The year 1988 should be propitious for reexamining U.S. attitudes and policies toward the Soviet Union—although, of course, election campaigns are rarely the best stage for the display of new ideas. It is necessary to think about the relationship for several reasons. One has just been indicated—the double divergence between the United States and its West Europeans allies. The second is the bankruptcy of current American diplomatic strategy. Under the very general guideline of containment, the United States has had periods with some kind of a strategic design (essentially 1947–1963, and 1969–1976) and periods without any (1963–1968, and 1977 to the present). Ten years in which policy toward the Soviet Union was, first, headed in two directions at once, and, subsequently, headed first in one direction, but mainly rhetorically and militarily, then in the opposite direction, but mainly on arms control, ought to be enough. In its declining years, the Reagan administration has shown signs of total inconsistency. It has resumed a political dialogue with Moscow and achieved some degree of cooperation with the Soviets in the Persian Gulf; yet it still justifies its naval buildup there in terms of the Soviet threat to the West's vital shipping lines, and still justifies its support for the contras in terms of the danger of another Soviet satellite in Central America just as the Soviets conditionally offer to cut their commitments to Nicaragua! A new political strategy has to be defined, one that takes into account the need to bring America's resources and commitments into greater balance. The third reason is the new Soviet course, which is still emerging, and which displays, if not radically different objectives, at least very different tactics and a new approach that shows the delayed impact of Western ideas (mutual security, interdependence, concentrating on what each side deems threatening, and the like) as well as a reappraisal of the value of adventures in the Third World. Gorbachev appears to represent much of the new generation of Soviet elites.

The circumstances seem to lend themselves to a major and sustained attempt at establishing a new relationship with Moscow. The unsteady and fluctuating contest of the past forty years reveals a trend behind the oscillations: a certain lowering of the intensity and narrowing of the scope of the Cold War. In Western Europe, the former core of the conflict, the principal remaining issue is the size and posture of the two opposing armies—not a minor problem, but one that can be addressed independently of underlying political tensions, since these have been largely resolved. Indeed, it is difficult to write credible scenarios in which such tensions would lead to war; the West Europeans are unlikely to rush to help rebellious East Europeans, and the Soviets and their allies have no incentive to invade a Federal Republic that accepts, however reluctantly, the division of the German nation and rejects nuclear weapons. In the so-called Third World, both the Soviet fling of the 1970s and the operations of the Reagan doctrine have resulted in parallel disillusionment. In the Middle East, both sides seem to prefer settlements to dangerous protracted conflicts. In the Far East, Soviet proposals, instead of trying to isolate China, aim at a reconciliation, and Soviet intermediate missiles will be destroyed. Both powers, as we have seen, have learned to fear nuclear war even more than each other. Neither power has, over forty years, obtained hegemony.

Indeed, the second favorable circumstance is the stark reality mentioned earlier—the economic strains on both superpowers. The U.S., with its budget and trade deficits, has become the world's greatest debtor country; its export structure shows the effects of a relative decline in its technological and industrial superiority. The country has been living beyond its means and risks losing control over its assets. The Soviet leader and his aides have eloquently described the quasi-bankruptcy of the Soviet system. Both countries need to concentrate on the domestic base of their external power—on education, on the economy, on social issues—and both need a respite from their wrestling match.

The third favorable circumstance is the Soviet new thinking, which emphasizes the demilitarization of world politics and mutuality and away from the boomerang effects of the traditional approach to world politics as a zero-sum game. It recognizes, if not multipolarity, at least the will to independence of nations with only a few more divisions than the Pope. It is willing to try to resolve regional conflicts through cooperation and to entangle the Soviet Union in international organizations and regimes—a switch, in other words, from mere peaceful coexistence to collaboration.[29]

A final favorable circumstance is a change in the American view of the Soviet Union. The public has a far more positive view of Gorbachev than of his predecessors. The elites used to perceive the Soviet Union as a strong state; later, in the 1970s, as a weak but dangerous state because all its strength was concentrated in the military, and its very rigidities, economic inefficiencies, and frustrations might incite it to seek a breakthrough via foreign adventure (the Imperial Germany misanalogy). Today, the Soviet Union is perceived as a weak state that has to rescue itself from decline through domestic reform. And while the Soviet regime is still perceived as totalitarian, there is a growing awareness of the fact that Soviet society, compressed and shaped by this regime, has nevertheless an often troubled life of its own.

Faced with Gorbachev's diplomatic blitz, American officials and commentators have often concentrated on somewhat marginal or irrelevant issues. They have praised or deplored his charm; they have wondered about his chances of survival at home (an interesting question, of course, but one we can't answer and that detracts attention from the question of what to do if he lasts). Another debate is about whether Gorbachev's proposals represent a real change or are merely a clever tactic aimed at undermining the West by appropriating Western notions and putting old ambitions in a new gard. The French have massively defended the second position, as have hardliners in the United States. But the fact is that there have been real changes—Soviet concessions in the INF and START negotiations that few Americans would have deemed likely in 1985. What matters is not the unlikely raising of a white flag or a conversion to what Arnold Wolfers called self-abnegation, but the nature of the strategy and tactics.

Thus, the essential problem for the United States is to define its own response to the new Soviet diplomacy, which requires reflection about what kind of Soviet foreign policy we ought to *want*, given the difficulty we face in trying to influence domestic developments in the Soviet Union directly (although we can affect them through our foreign and military policies), and also given the requirement that we be realistic about what we *can*, at best, hope for.

For what is not an option, clearly, is the course that the architects of containment—and of the détente of the 1970s—had devised: bringing Moscow to the point where the Soviet leaders would deem it in their interest to behave as the government of a "moderate" nonrevolutionary power resigned to a stable world order defined and dominated by Washington, renounce turbulence and activism beyond its imperial sphere, and perhaps even allow some emancipation of its satellites in that sphere. This vision of a world in which what is ours is ours and what is theirs is negotiable is simply not achievable. To be sure, the new Soviet course may create the illusion that peaceful victory through strength has been won by the West. The priority given by Gorbachev to domestic "restructuring" and to increasing economic efficiency suggests that Soviet behavior will be restrained, but such restraint doesn't mean retrenchment or passivity. Gail Lapidus, indeed, gives a very "Gaullist" interpretation of Gorbachev's strategy[30] as the one that aims not only at providing the goods the Soviet peoples want but also at keeping the Soviet Union from falling behind in the world race. It seeks to extricate the Soviet Union from dead-end positions without jeopardizing existing alliances and to revive atrophied diplomatic instruments unused by Gromyko in order to increase, not reduce, Soviet influence abroad. One of the challenges Gorbachev poses for the United States is this: Americans have ritually asked for changes in Soviet external behavior, with the explicit hope or tacit expectation that more moderate behavior would mean a decreased Soviet role in the world. What happens if greater moderation actually means a less aggressive strategy but a more active and effective Soviet diplomacy?

The terms of the American debate may well change. It used to be a clash between those who wanted the Soviet Union to behave more like a status quo power and those who thought that we should tolerate their support of revolutionary or anti-Western forces in areas of limited importance as long as no overt aggression was involved: the competition would thus remain for ideological predominance but at lower levels of intensity and violence. Now, we may be faced with a reduced level both of violence and of ideological intensity, but also with a heightened diplomatic activism, aimed not at installing Communist regimes or even "progressive" ones but at encouraging independence from Washington, the development of a plurality of centers of power. This is precisely what Americans often present as *their* goal, yet have not unfrequently discouraged. For the first time in thirty-five years, there certainly is a danger posed by the new diplomatic skills of the Soviets. Not since Stalin's last attempts at keeping Bonn out of NATO have there been so many initiatives, most of which indeed throw back at the West ideas that it originated but that (like the zero option or proposals for extensive verifications) Moscow had always rejected in the past.

Given this new and very different challenge, the U.S. has a choice between two policies. One would consist in acting as if there had been no change at all. The report called *Discriminate Deterrence*, signed by such luminaries as Henry Kissinger, Zbigniew Brzezinski, Fred Iklé, Albert Wohlstetter, and Samuel Huntington, is a perfect example of an effort that claims to address the realities of a world in which the more extreme scenarios of Soviet aggression are the least likely, yet fails in any way to question its omnipresent, underlying hypothesis—that of a relentless, largely military (if prudent) Soviet drive for world domination. The result is a kind of unselective paranoia, or a high-tech version of NSC 68, in contradiction with trends not only in Soviet policy but also in the Third World (where the report proposes to find clients that will fight for our cause), unacceptable to many of our allies, unsustainable at home (there is no price tag), often morally objectionable, and likely, if carried out, to effect a self-fulfilling prophecy in our relations with Moscow.

The other policy is one of competing boldly with Gorbachev on the terrain he himself has chosen, and that is the ground we ourselves have proposed. This does not mean making concessions in order to help him, unless they are in the interest of the West and matched by Soviet concessions; payments in advance are usually disastrous. However, there may well be, for the first time, a major convergence of interests on serious arms control measures, aimed not merely at reducing numbers, but at restructuring forces so as to remove, in the nuclear realm, any incentive to a first strike—to consolidate crisis stability— and, in the conventional field, so as to diminish the offensive capabilities of the two coalitions in the heart of Europe (where the Warsaw Pact's tanks are poised for a breakthrough, and NATO experiments with a counteroffensive strategy of its own). A chance exists for discussions on the military doctrines of the two sides, on confidence-building measures, and on changes in deployments that would make a surprise attack less likely. There appears to be, at least, a realization in Moscow that the Soviet-American dialogue cannot be isolated from the so-called movement of social forces in the Third World, or rather that U.S.–Soviet cooperation is at the mercy of confrontations there between Moscow (or its allies) and the United States (or its proxies).

It is therefore necessary for the U.S. to revitalize its own, often sluggish diplomacy (including in the U.N.), to try to negotiate with

Moscow in order to "smoke out" Gorbachev, insofar as his strategy is still ambiguous, and in order to attract him ever more deeply into the field of action he tells us he has chosen. Thus, we ought to engage Moscow in a process or resolution of those regional disputes in which both sides still have considerable influence—as has happened over Afghanistan, and should happen in the various Middle Eastern conflicts and over the issue of external interventions in Central America. On conventional arms control, NATO needs to test tantalizing Soviet hints about "sufficiency," the elimination of asymmetries and a move to defensive postures, by making proposals of its own. In the nuclear realm, the kind of deal that the START negotiators have been aiming at—50 percent reductions on offensive arms (with the right ratios of warheads to targets) and the preservation of the ABM treaty (with an agreement on acceptable tests of the components of defensive systems)—remains the best immediate goal. The Western goal in both sets of arms negotiations ought to be military de-escalation without undermining nuclear deterrence, which means reducing the importance of nuclear weapons in world affairs and in arsenals because (as Gorbachev has proclaimed)[31] they are unusable, and reducing the size and the threats represented by the two military coalitions in Europe, and also giving up talk about denuclearization to be achieved either by abolishing all nuclear weapons or through perfect defenses.

Thus, Gorbachev's challenge is also an opportunity. Usually, as Paul Kennedy has written, declining hegemonic powers are confronted with rising foreign challenges that oblige them to increase their military expenses, and thus to slash their productive investments, reduce growth, raise taxes, and split their public. This time, the Soviets are the ones who complain that the United States is forcing the Soviet Union to arm itself to economic death.[32] Neither side is a Sparta threatened by the rise of Athens: the process under way is what Pierre Hassner once called competitive decadence. There is a common interest in decreasing the burden of defense. Moreover, a Soviet Union that relies primarily on its own internal efforts so as to become a modern great power might be less eager to obtain its certificate of superpower legitimacy from joint U.S.S.R.–U.S. declarations or treaties that run into American objections to condominium. Such a change might allow for pragmatic, case by case, political consultations and understandings. There would still be American reluctance to consecrating a Soviet role in Western *"chasses gardées;"* but the persistence of such an attitude would play into Soviet hands and allow the new Soviet leadership to arouse the anti-American resentments of countries that do not want to be the political satellites of Washington even if they often do not mind being its military protégés.

Grasping the Gorbachev opportunity would still leave, and create, headaches for the United States. One obstacle is created by the continuing difference in designs. I am not referring to the argument that Gorbachev's objectives remain all the traditional subversive or destabilizing Soviet aims—for instance, the denuclearization of Western Europe, or the creation of as much trouble as possible between the U.S. and its European allies. It may well be that Moscow's ultimate goals have not changed, and it is true that on many issues (including the meaning of sufficiency in defense, and the conventional balance of Europe) Soviet positions are undefined, marked by contradictions, fluctuations, and lags between the leader's bold slogans and the bureaucratic machine. But ultimate goals, as George Kennan once wrote,[33] are "normally vainglorious, unreal, extravagant, even pathetic—little likely to be realized, scarcely to be taken seriously. . . . Methods (are) another matter. . . . It (is) out of their immediate effects that the quality of life (is) really molded." And it is precisely in the realm of methods—of how to move toward the hazy goals—that changes are visible. There is a world of difference between the quest for influence through bullying and aggression, and the same quest through diplomatic maneuver and rewards. As for the hesitations and gaps, our own responses can contribute to their elimination.

The real problem is elsewhere: the Soviet design, whether it still aims or not at "world hegemony" or the triumph of communism, clearly seeks to increase Soviet influence, albeit by gentler means; and the U.S. is unlikely to resign itself to this. There may be a revision of the Leninist model and ideology in Moscow, but Gorbachev is a true believer in the virtues of Leninist Socialism. The U.S., on the other hand, remains deeply hostile to the Soviet regime and to the Leninist ideal, and the ideological blend that emerged in this country in the years after World War II has not lost its potency, even if the superpower contest has become less virulent. The Soviet design for a Soviet-dominated, Communist world order may well have been (tacitly) discarded; but the Soviet desire for a greater role in the world (even if it is through deals with established governments rather than through help to revolutionaries) is still there. The American desire for influence is equally strong and the desire for a scheme of world order along the familiar Wilsonian lines has not been discarded at all.

There are formidable external obstacles as well. Many of the regional issues that can't be solved without the superpowers remain intractable even when they agree, and the positions and interests of the two countries often remain divergent. Reductions in their military arsenals may spur nuclear proliferation, which even closer U.S.–Soviet cooperation may not be able to stop. And there are difficult issues in the European arena. The INF agreement puts the spotlight back on conventional defense, but a shrinkage of NATO's conventional forces (American as well as European) is more likely than an increase;[34] it would be dangerous to count on being rescued by Soviet offers of mutual reductions, not only because this would make of the Soviet Union NATO's *deus ex machina*, but also because (as the French point out) the Soviets, however much they cut, rearrange, or pull back, have a built-in geographical advantage and might want to exploit their reductions to achieve a further removal of those American nuclear forces in Europe that threaten East European and Soviet territory, but that are essential for the preservation of the NATO nuclear deterrent threat. The negotiation on conventional forces will be complicated by the number of participants, and by the difficulty of distinguishing offensive from defensive weapons, and by the conflicts of interest and military doctrines among NATO members. And while NATO prepares for negotiations and begins to bargain, it risks being torn between advocates of force modernization and force increases to put NATO into a better bargaining position, and opponents who argue that such measures would backfire by making agreement more difficult. Both in the nuclear realm after INF and in the conventional one, NATO faces the difficult task of making its strategy and its arms control policies compatible. For as the American nuclear arsenal in and around Europe shrinks, the credibility of a deterrent threat aimed at compensating for Soviet conventional superiority shrinks too.

Finally, there are domestic obstacles in both countries. In the Soviet Union, the military have not yet adjusted their thinking to Gorbachev's. Moreover, he could fail, either because of domestic opposition or because his new policies provoke, in Eastern Europe or at home, the kind of turbulence that would force him to change his course. In the U.S., distrust of the Soviet Union remains deep, whatever the image of Gorbachev himself. The election campaign of 1988 demonstrated both the persistence of suspicion and the reluctance of candidates to break out of the Cold War mold. Even though the conditions are very different from those of the early 1970s—when each side interpreted détente as a way of tying up the rival, whereas the realities of today point to a slowdown (at least) of the arms race and to a less bipolar world—the idea of a new détente, purged of the illusions of the earlier one, remains unwelcome to politicians who remember what happened to the last one. The institutional obstacles described above are as powerful as ever. They combine with strong intellectual or ideological habits to delay, if not prevent, a clear realization of the fact that the "American century" is over. How many of America's leaders and officials understand that America's (like the Soviet Union's) best chance for maximizing influence is not devolution, which means the transfer of burdens and responsibilities to others in a common enterprise whose strategy is still defined by the United States, and certainly not domination, but the exploitation of opportunities in a complex, fragmented, and therefore far less manageable world—the very thing Americans most dislike facing?

In the long run, and whatever happens in Moscow, neither power will have the resources and the ability to dominate world politics as in the past. The limits on the productivity of force, which effect the superpowers especially, the rise of major new economic actors, of regional middle powers, all suggest a much more crowded field and complex game of nations with perils of its own. The Cold War, for all the crises it bred, also created a measure of stability and predictability; the new game instills uncertainty in the alliance systems, is riddled with largely autonomous and self-sustaining local quarrels, and risks reverting to widespread economic conflict and chaos.

In relations with Moscow, the ultimate choice for the United States seems to be between a mechanical pursuit of traditional containment, whose primary instrument is a military buildup that appears increasingly ruinous and futile—even strongly anti-Soviet leaders feel the need to limit the risks of an eventual resort to force—and a very different policy that would aim at demilitarizing the contest as much as possible and bringing to the foreground of world politics all those nonbipolar aspects that have been ignored, pushed back, or played down. To what extent this will be possible depends only in part on Moscow. Insofar as Washington is concerned, what would be required over time is the acceptance of a transformation of NATO into an alliance between the U.S. and a Western European entity engaged in the difficult endeavor of assuming primary responsibility for its conventional defense and of playing a much greater role than in the past in nuclear deterrence as well. What would also be required is a redefinition of the expectations in the Soviet-American rivalry, which will continue: not victory (either at Armageddon—which would be suicidal—or through Soviet resignation to playing a part in the orchestra we conduct), but a contest for influence in which we would do better than they through superior economic assets and diplomatic skills—a contest that, by involving Moscow more deeply in world affairs, might gradually combine with trends in Soviet society to produce more than cosmetic changes in the Soviet regime itself.

The superstars who have dominated the stage have gotten older, relatively poorer, and are surrounded by younger actors. One of the aging Thespians seems to have noticed. Will the American one follow suit?

Notes

1. Theodore Draper, "American Hubris: From Truman to the Persian Gulf," *New York Review of Books*, July 16, 1987, pp. 40–48.
2. I have developed this more fully in *Gulliver's Troubles* (New York: McGraw Hill, 1968). See also Michael H. Hunt, *Ideology and U.S. Foreign Policy* (New Haven: Yale University Press, 1987)—an incisive analysis that reaches provocative (and debatable) conclusions.
3. To be sure, he was not entirely consistent, as his interventions in Mexico and Central America show!
4. See his *Russia, the Soviet Union and the United States* (New York: John Wiley, 1978), chapter V.
5. In George F. Kennan, *Memoirs 1925–1950* (Boston: Little, Brown, 1967), pp. 550 and 548.
6. *Ideology and Foreign Policy*, chapter 5, cited above.
7. In chapter 6 of *The Long Peace* (New York: Oxford University Press, 1987).
8. See their chapter in Kenneth A. Oye, Robert J. Lieber, and Donald Rothchild, *Eagle Defiant* (Boston: Little, Brown, 1983), pp. 191–236.
9. See, for instance, my analysis in *Janus and Minerva* (Boulder, Colorado: Westview, 1986), chapter 11.
10. See his *Theory of International Politics* (Reading: Addison-Wesley, 1979).
11. John L. Gaddis, *The Long Peace*, chapter 5, cited above.
12. See the complex analysis by Richard Betts, *Nuclear Blackmail and Nuclear Balance* (Washington: Brookings, 1987).
13. *Russia, the Soviet Union and the United States*, pp. 209–210, cited above.
14. Michael Mandelbaum, "Western Influence on the Soviet Union," in Seweryn Bialer and Michael Mandelbaum, editors, *Gorbachev's Russia and American Foreign Policy* (Boulder, Colorado: Westview Press, 1988).
15. See Paul Stockton, *Strategic Stability Between the Superpowers*, Adelphi Papers No. 213, Winter 1986.
16. "Nuclear Learning and U.S.–Soviet Security Regimes," *International Organization*, vol. 41, no. 3 (Summer 1987), pp. 371–402.
17. "Superpower Ethics: The Rules of the Game," *Ethics and International Affairs*, vol. I (1987), pp. 37–51.

18. Robert Gilpin, "American Policy in the Post-Reagan Era," *Daedalus*, vol. 116, no. 3 (Summer 1987), pp. 33–68. Paul Kennedy, "The (Relative) Decline of America," *The Atlantic*, August 1987, pp. 29–38. Samuel P. Huntington struggles, somewhat inconclusively, with the issue in "Coping with the Lippman Gap," *Foreign Affairs, America and the World 1987–88*, pp. 453–477.

19. See in particular Tom Farer's introduction to a forthcoming collection of his essays, *The Grand Strategy of the United States in Latin America* (New Brunswick, N.J.: Transaction Books).

20. See my analysis, "Détente," in Joseph S. Nye, Jr., ed., *The Making of America's Soviet Policy* (New Haven: Yale University Press, for the Council on Foreign Relations, 1984), pp. 231–264; and Raymond L. Garthoff's exhaustive *Détente and Confrontation* (Washington: Brookings, 1985), especially chapters 29 and 30.

21. *American Public Opinion and U.S. Foreign Policy 1987* (Chicago: Chicago Council on Foreign Relations, 1987). I have relied on analyses by William Schneider, Andrew Kohut, and Richard Smoke.

22. *Russia, the Soviet Union and the United States*, p. 168, cited above.

23. "The Cold War," in Nye, *The Making of America's Soviet Policy*, (fn. 16), pp. 209–230.

24. There is one exception: the farmers' lobby—not in domestic terms, a left-leaning force, but one whose interest in grain deals with the Soviet Union led Reagan to lift the grain embargo imposed by Carter after Afghanistan.

25. *Mortal Rivals* (New York: Random House, 1987), p. 55.

26. *Ibid*, pp. 161 and 216.

27. *The Long Peace*, chapter 3.

28. *Discriminate Deterrence* (Report of the Commission on Long-Term Integrated Strategy, January 1988), p. 27.

29. See *How Should America Respond to Gorbachev's Challenge?* (Report of the Task Force on Soviet New Thinking, Institute for East-West Security Studies, New York, 1987), pp. 17–18.

30. "Gorbachev and the Reform of the Soviet System," *Daedalus*, vol. 116, no. 2 (Spring 1987), pp. 1–30. I have also relied on unpublished papers by Robert Legvold and Seweryn Bialer.

31. *Perestroika* (New York: Harper & Row, 1987), p. 219.

32. See, for instance, a recent speech by Yakovlev, mentioned in Soviet–East European Report, vol. IV, no. 34, September 13, 1987.

33. *Memoirs 1925–1950*, p. 199, cited above.

34. See, for instance, Christopher Bertram, "Europe's Security Dilemma," *Foreign Affairs*, (Summer 1987), pp. 942–957.

Council on Foreign Relations
Conference on Western Attitudes
Toward the Soviet Union
September 28-29, 1987

Stanley Hoffmann, Chairman and author - Harvard University
Michael E. Mandelbaum, Group Director - Council on Foreign Relations
Pierre Hassner, Author - Fondation Nationale des Sciences Politiques
Edwina Moreton, Author -*The Economist*
Gregory Treverton, Author - Council on Foreign Relations
Cynthia B. Paddock, Rapporteur - Council on Foreign Relations

Madeleine Albright - Georgetown University
Deanne Arsenian - Carnegie Corporation
James Chace - Carnegie Endowment for International Peace
James W. Davis, Jr. - Council onForeign Relations
Lynn Davis - International Institute of Strategic Studies
Kempton Dunn - Council on Foreign Relations
Toby Trister Gati - UN Association of the USA
William H. Gleysteen, Jr. - Council on Foreign Relations
Lincoln Gordon - Brookings Institution
Judith Gustafson - Council on Foreign Relations
William G. Hyland - *Foreign Affairs*
Tamar Jacoby - *Newsweek*
Clifford Krauss - Visiting Edward R. Murrow Press Fellow
Colonel Stanley Kwieciak, Jr., U. S. Army - Visiting Military Fellow
F. Stephen Larrabee - Institute for East-West Security Studies
Kathleen Troia McFarland - formerly of The Defense Department
Steven J. Monde - Council on Foreign Relations
David Morey - East-West Forum
Enid C. B. Schoettle - Ford Foundation
Colette Shulman - Columbia University
John Temple Swing - Council on Foreign Relations
Peter Tarnoff - Council on Foreign Relations
William Taubman - Amherst College
Nicholas Wahl - New York University

About the Authors

Pierre Hassner is Research Director at the Centre d'Etudes et de Recherches Internationales, Fondation Nationale des Science Politiques in Paris. He is the author of numerous works in French and English, including contributions to Sarah Meiklejohn Terry, editor, *Soviet Policy in Eastern Europe*, and Lincoln Gordon, editor, *Eroding Empire*.

Stanley Hoffmann is Douglas Dillon Professor of the Civilization of France at Harvard University. Among the many books of which he is the author or co-author are *Janus and Minerva* and *The Mitterand Experiment*.

Edwina Moreton is a member of the editorial staff of *The Economist* and writes on Soviet and East European affairs, Germany, China, and East-West relations.

Gregory F. Treverton is Senior Fellow at the Council on Foreign Relations where he directs the Europe-American Project. His most recent books are *Making the Alliance Work: The United States and Western Europe*, and *Covert Action: The Limits of Intervention in the Postwar World*.

Michael Mandelbaum is Director of the Project on East-West Relations and Senior Fellow at the Council on Foreign Relations. He is the author, most recently, of *The Fate of Nations: The Search for National Security in the Nineteenth and Twentieth Centuries* and, with Seweryn Bialer, *The Global Rivals*.